THE MANAGER'S POCKET GUIDE TO
SYSTEMS THINKING
& LEARNING

by Stephen G. Haines

HRD PRESS
Amherst, Massachusetts

Published by:
HRD Press
22 Amherst Road
Amherst, MA 01002
1-800-822-2801 (U.S. and Canada)
1-413-253-3488
1-413-253-3499 (Fax)
http://www.hrdpress.com

ISBN 0-87425-453-1

Cover design by Eileen Klockars
Production services by CompuDesign
Editorial services by Mary George

Printed in Canada

TABLE OF CONTENTS

— CONCLUSION —

INTRODUCTION

The purpose of this guidebook is to provide progressive managers with practical tools for enhancing learning, change, and performance on individual, team, and organizational levels. The design and content of these tools are based on systems thinking and learning, a way of thought, understanding, and action that offers each of us a better means to achieve the results we desire.

FROM THEORY TO AUTHENTIC PRACTICE

Systems thinking comes from a rigorous scientific discipline called General Systems Theory, which developed from the study of biology in the 1920s. The theory centered on the natural world, the living systems there-in, and the common laws governing those systems. Its major premise was that such laws, once known, could serve as a conceptual framework for understanding the relationships within any system, and for handling any problems or changes encompassed by that system. Consequently, the theory emphasized the value of viewing a system as a whole, of gaining a perspective on the entire "entity" before examining its parts. It is this emphasis that informs and shapes the practice of systems thinking—the *authentic* kind, the kind we will be concerned with in this book.

Authenticity is an important point because the term *systems* thinking has risen into popular use—a result of the practice's major role in Peter Senge's bestseller *The Fifth Discipline*—and, as an organizational-change buzzword, it is often applied indiscriminately. People use *systems thinking* (and *systems learning* as well) to cover a broad range of meanings, from anything that links up with something else to a list of topics that all relate to training, education, and achieving change. This overgeneralization not only undermines the distinct power of systems thinking but also brings into question whether most people know what the word *system* even means.

To clarify matters from the start, here are the definitions essential to the use of authentic systems thinking, and on which the contents of this guidebook are based.

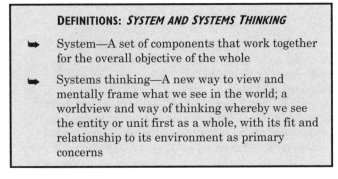

DEFINITIONS: *SYSTEM AND SYSTEMS THINKING*

➡ System—A set of components that work together for the overall objective of the whole

➡ Systems thinking—A new way to view and mentally frame what we see in the world; a worldview and way of thinking whereby we see the entity or unit first as a whole, with its fit and relationship to its environment as primary concerns

The connection of systems thinking to General Systems Theory is evident in the above definition. Whatever happened to the theory itself? It never made the leap into mainstream consciousness, and thus became a lost art— at least until now.

FROM CHAOS AND COMPLEXITY TO ELEGANT SIMPLICITY

In this book, the secrets of General Systems Theory—its perceptions of the natural world around us, its framework and characteristics—have been rediscovered and put into practical tools for success in today's chaotic and complex world. I've taken these natural laws and organized them into four categories:

1. The Seven Levels of Living (Open) Systems

2. The Laws of Natural Systems: Standard Systems Dynamics

3. The A-B-C-D Systems Model

4. Changing Systems: The Natural Cycles of Life and Change

Each category represents an *elegantly simple* concept that, in conjunction with the others, gives us an invaluable framework for viewing the world and its systems. By adopting this new perspective, we can bring order and re-finement to our understanding of those systems, thus im-proving our ability to problem-solve and effect needed changes within them.

SYSTEMS THINKING: A NEW ORIENTATION TO LIFE

For over 20 years I have seen firsthand just how useful the systems thinking framework is as an orientation to life. In my younger, military days I was trained in engineering—a discipline grounded in analytical and reductionist thinking—and so the framework came as quite a revelation to me. It has since helped me become more successful in my career, first as a senior corporate executive and then as a CEO and consultant to CEOs. And it can help you become more successful too.

Why is systems thinking so effective as an orientation to life? Because it is based on a simple but profound truth:

Living systems are the natural order of life. Most of us, however, overlook this truth; we tend to take natural and universal laws for granted, rather than explore their secrets to see what they can teach us about life and our perceptions of the world. It is an unfortunate tendency, and one I hope to help remedy through the tools in this guidebook.

So get ready for a new orientation to life—for an elegantly simple way to view the world and better understand the dynamics of its systems. Let systems thinking and learning clarify and simplify how you see reality, so you too can operate more successfully in today's complex and globally interconnect world. Here's to elegant simplicity . . . and to systems solutions!

1. Understanding Systems Thinking & Learning

A new age—the Systems Age—has clearly begun. Today's technological changes and innovations focus mainly on systems, particularly electronic ones, and on systems linking and interface (e.g., GATT, Mercosur, the Internet). The systems around us have multiplied and enlarged, often to overwhelming numbers and proportions. Corporations span the globe; communications satellites ring the skies. As distance is redefined, systems collide in countless ways, defying our comprehension of change and the adequacy our usual problem-solving methods. We find ourselves in a small world of enormous complexity, a new world that demands we see it from a new perspective—a systems perspective—with a mindset attuned to processes, patterns, and relationships. Systems thinking is tailor-made to meet this demand and to help us manage our organizations in the Systems Age.

DISCOVERING THE SYSTEMS THINKING MINDSET

To begin with, we must understand that any mindset consists of mental models, or concepts, that influence our interpretation of situations and predispose us to certain responses. These models, which are replete with beliefs and assumptions, thus strongly determine the way we understand the world and act in it. The irony is, they become so ingrained in us, as tendencies and predispositions, that we seldom pay attention to them. Even when something in our experience calls them into question—an "unsolvable" problem, perhaps, or an "unmanagable" interpersonal conflict—we miss the call. Those problems and conflicts, patched up for the time being, never really get resolved, and we wonder why success eludes us.

Often, not until a crisis hits, driving us deep into ourselves, do we realize we've been acting on unfounded beliefs or outmoded assumptions, and finally shift our mindset. But we don't always catch the obvious lesson: that we need to put ourselves in touch with our mental models, hold them up to the light and look for biases and unsupported "facts," those things which cause us to *mis*understand the world; in short, that we must take an active role in shaping our mindsets, opting for mental models which better "capture" the world we need to understand. It is at this point where the systems thinking mindset comes in.

Mindset and Worldview

The beauty of this mindset is that its mental models are based on natural laws, principles of interrelationship, and interdependence found in all living systems. They give us a new view of ourselves and our many systems, from the tiniest cell to the entire earth; and as our organizations are included in that great range, they help us define organizational problems as systems problems, so we can respond in more productive ways. The systems thinking mindset is a new orientation to life. In many ways it also operates as a *worldview*—an overall perspective on, and understanding of, the world.

To develop this mindset, we must first look to three fundamental principles of living systems: that of openness, interrelationship, and interdependence.

The Principle of Openness

Any system falls into one of two basic categories: open or closed. An *open system* accepts inputs from its environment, acts on the inputs to create outputs, and releases the outputs to its environment. In contrast, a *closed system* is isolated and hermetic; an experimental, sterile chemistry lab would be an example. Virtually every system in which we operate is an open system, although some are more open than others—a key to success, as we shall see later in this guidebook.

By viewing the systems around us as open ones, we become more aware of their interactions with their environment. This awareness is crucial, for if we are to manage change, make decisions, and solve problems within systems, our considerations *must* include that environment as well as the systems components that support the objective of the whole. This is the nature of systems, and we have to work with it.

The Principles of Interrelationship and Interdependence

When one component of a system changes, it affects many other systems components and may even alter the entire system. Likewise, when a system itself changes, it has a necessary effect on the other systems in its environment. Why? Because there are points of relationship and interdependence that extend through and across systems and link them in various ways.

Just think of an ecosystem like a salt marsh. Its inhabitants—biological systems such as birds, insects, mollusks, grasses, algae—depend on the conditions of that marsh; but the conditions also depend on them. If the grasses begin to die off, for example, the birds will be more vulnerable to intruders and have no place to nest; their absence will cause condition breakdown for other inhabitants, who will likely overpopulate; moreover, the lack of grasses will mean more erosion. If poor conditions continue, eventually the marsh will be little more than a drainage hole.

Why might the grasses begin to die? Because of a change in the marsh's environment, in other systems. Maybe an increase in storms has resulted in a closed breechway, causing water deoxygenation (a causal chain running from weather to coastal to marshland systems); or perhaps or a rise in beach traffic has lead to more exhaust pollutants (a confluence of chemical, technological and biological systems). And the loss of the marsh will affect the entire coastal area, itself a system full of systems and interrelated with, and interdependent on, its environmental systems.

The above is, of course, a worst-case scenario, yet we see similar scenarios all the time, and not only in ecological systems. We see them in the failure of businesses, communities, and even nations; these too are living systems, part of the natural order of life. We also see them in ourselves, for we are biological entities, each body a configuration of physical and mental systems. Our overall well-being is inextricably bound up in the well-being of those systems, with patterns of interdependence linking them to one another and their environment. Just how strong these links are becomes clearer all the time. We now know, for instance, that mental stress can compromise the immune system and that an optimistic attitude can help the body heal faster. Because neither stress nor optimism can be looked at under a microscope, this relationship strikes some people as odd, even dubious; but to someone with a systems thinking mindset, it makes complete sense—is simply the laws of living systems at work.

Putting the Principles to Work

Once we get a mental handle on the principles of openness, interrelationship, and interdependence, it is only natural

> ➤ **"SEEING" EARTH: A SYSTEMS MINDSET EXERCISE**

To grasp the marvelous "fabric" of systems, mentally stand back for a moment from your life, your work, your city, state, nation, world. Think of the NASA photographs of Earth—find one in a book, if possible—and imagine you are out in space, seeing our blue and white planet shining in the immense blackness.

Does Earth seem isolated and independent to you? If so, *shift your perspective.* Think of the solar system and the gravitational force exerted by the sun and the planets and their moons. Consider the distribution of matter across the planets, the basic structure of the atoms which link that matter, the force which holds atoms and molecules together. Imagine, if you can, that suddenly, in one area of the solar system—say the area around Jupiter—there is a breakdown in those forces. What happens to Earth? *Does it seem as isolated and independent anymore?*

Now focus on Earth itself. Think about the statement "Earth is a chaotic mess of unrelated and isolated events, conditions, and living things." Does this statement make sense? How could you disprove it simply by *looking* at our planet? Does its blueness and whiteness (its seas and atmosphere) and its shine (reflectivity) indicate unrelatedness and isolation? Do these features rely only on themselves for their existence? What else do they rely on? And what relies on them? Would the statement "Earth is a single, complex organism" make far more sense? Why? What does it imply?

for us to wonder how we can get a practical handle on putting them to work in our organizations and other living systems. The fact is, many of us have already begun to do it. Collaborative, team, and systems-oriented efforts are becoming more and more common in organizations and communities. Also, there are fields of thought such as Gestalt Therapy, Complexity Theory, and Chaos Theory, and technological areas like operations research, tele-communications, and information systems, that deal with the interrelationship of processes and patterns—*the art of systems thinking in its broadest sense.* Among its practitioners are such diverse people as Fritjoff Capra, Jay Forester, Peter Senge, Russ Ackoff, Meg Wheatley, Eric Trist, and Ludwig von Bertalanffy, all of whom recognize that systems behave in accordance with these principles, and that what we see changing on one systems level will affect other levels in various, ongoing patterns of cause and effect.

To become practitioners of that art ourselves, we need to start looking at societal and organizational problems as *systems problems* and seek systems-integrated solutions. Rather than identify a problem as one isolated occurrence, we must learn to identify and solve *patterns of problems.* We also must try to detect patterns of relationship and interdependence between systems, looking for "leverage points"—areas of influence that, if acted upon, can lead to lasting beneficial changes throughout those systems.

Our systems thinking mindset thus requires mental models that help us discover more than just "partial systems" solutions—what we tend to get in today's systems-focused efforts. As yet there is only one body of thought that provides us with those mental models, offering us a way to reach fully integrated solutions to our systems problems. And it is not Gestalt Therapy or Chaos Theory. *It is General Systems Theory,* a lost art based on a natural perspective of the world and its many systems. Perhaps because its originators were primarily biologists, this theory looks not to artificial constructs or paradigms for its understanding of the world, but to life itself, acknowledging that living systems are the natural order of life. Let's take a closer look.

GENERAL SYSTEMS THEORY

In the 1920s, biologist Ludwig von Bertalanffy and others proposed the idea of a general theory of systems that would embrace all levels of science, from the study of a single cell to the study of society and the planet as a whole. They were seeking these generalizations in order to create a recognizable standard of scientific principles that could then be applied to virtually any body of work. Out of this study came the scientific application called General Systems Theory.

Geoffrey Vickers, in 1970, explained the theory more in layman's terms:

> *The words general systems theory imply that some things can usefully be said about systems in general, despite the immense diversity of their specific forms. One of these things should be a scheme of classification.*

> *Every science begins by classifying its subject matter, if only descriptively, and learns a lot about it in the process . . Systems especially need this attention, because an adequate classification cuts across familiar boundaries and at the same time draws valid and important distinctions which have previously been sensed but not defined.*

> *In short, the task of General Systems Theory is to find the most general conceptual framework in which a scientific theory or a technological problem can be placed without losing the essential features of the theory or the problem.*

This theory, then, is a marvelous vehicle for framing and describing universal relationships. Its basic precept is that, in our work on any problem, the whole should be our primary consideration, with the parts secondary. The theory also states that parts play their role in light of the purpose for which the whole exists—no part can be affected without affecting all other parts. Thus, when we want to study any system, be it organizational, organic, or scientific in nature, we must begin at the right place.

The place to start is with the whole.

All parts of the whole—and their relationships to one another—evolve from this.

This conceptual approach is therefore quite different from our familiar reductionist, analytic, and mechanistic ways of thinking—ones whose age has come and gone. Moving beyond them won't be easy, but it can be done.

SYSTEMS THINKING VERSUS "MACHINE AGE" THINKING

In *The Fifth Discipline,* Peter Senge succinctly captures the situation we're faced with. He states:

> *From an early age, we're taught to break apart problems in order to make complex tasks and subjects easier to deal with. But this creates a bigger problem . . . we lose the ability to see the consequences of our actions, and we lose a sense of connection to a larger whole.*

When did this "lesson" take hold in our society? Quite possibly in the Agricultural Age. Many social theorists believe that today's problems stem from that age, when we found ways to dominate nature and make it subservient to our immediate needs. The Industrial Revolution furthered that dominating mode, as it was a "mechanistic revolution" fueled by the intent to take over and conquer Mother Nature. And it worked—or so we thought.

The mechanistic approach to effecting change is no longer viable, if it ever was. As Russell Ackoff reminds us, "We [have been] attempting to deal with problems generated by a new [systems] age with techniques and tools that we inherit from an old [mechanistic] one." Ackoff believes these old techniques and tools developed as the Agricultural Age closed and the Machine Age began. In his view, the latter spawned three fundamental concepts: reductionism, analysis, and mechanization. He further believes they now must change if we want to be in step with the Systems Age.

The Fundamental Concepts of the Machine Age

1. Reductionism. This concept's premise is that if you take anything and start to take it apart, or reduce it to its lowest common denominator, you will ultimately reach indivisible elements. For instance, in reductionism, the cell would be the ultimate component of life.

2. Analysis. A powerful mode of thinking, analysis takes the entity/issue/problem apart, breaking it up into its components. At that point in analysis, you would solve the problem, then aggregate the solutions into an explanation as a whole. Analysis tends to explain things by the behavior of their parts, not the whole!

Even today, analysis is probably the most common technique used in corporations. Managers "cut their problems down to size," reducing them to a set of solvable components and then assembling them into a solution as a whole. *It is still so much the norm that many continue to see analyzing as synonymous with thinking.* Instead, synthesis or holistic systems thinking is what's required.

3. Mechanization. This seeks to explain virtually every phenomenon by resorting to a single relationship: cause and effect. However, mechanization has a key consequence:

when we find the cause, we believe we don't need anything else, so the environment becomes irrelevant. Indeed, the whole effort of scientific study is about relationships that can be studied in isolation and in laboratories—a closed-systems view of the world.

Mechanization colored how we looked the world as a whole. It brought us assembly lines, mass production, countless machines—and the idea that we live in a mechanistic, rather than organic, world. We have gone from thinking of machines as a means for mass production to thinking of the whole world as a machine, not as "Mother Nature," with a will and a mind of her own.

Appearance and Reality

While the reductionist, analytic, and mechanistic approaches may appear to resolve ongoing problems, they actually fail to provide long-term, permanent solutions. Analytic thinking is perhaps the biggest culprit among them, for it is such a common way of thinking that we're hardly aware of doing it. Because its central, linear approach is to problem-solve only one issue at a time, other issues must wait their turn, and this alone can cause problems. It's the inherent deficiency of this thinking mode—something important to remember and be on the alert for.

Simple analytic thinking focuses on cause-and-effect: one cause for every one effect. It asks the all too common either/or question. Its weakest link, and the reason it's not working in today's world, is that it doesn't take into consideration the environment, other systems, and the multiple and/or delayed causality that surrounds each cause and effect. Nor does it consider a part's interrelationships and interdependencies with other parts.

Analytic thinking, when paired with reductionism, does makes us "micro-smart"—that is, good at thinking through individual projects and elements—but it also makes us "macro-dumb" at planning for the whole portfolio. Here are a few dramatic examples of how analytic thinking has run amuck and led to needless complexity.

- *The U.S. Naval Academy Regulations*—Over 1000 pages, as compared to 10 pages when the Academy opened 150 years ago. Both versions cover the same topics, but whereas the earlier one assumes readers can apply common sense, the other spells out each and every probability.

- *Heath Care*—Thousands of small, specialized programs, often based on grants created for singular, simplistic problems and solutions

- *Specialized Government Districts*—Thousands of unaccountable districts: water districts, assessment districts, school districts, and so forth

- *Federal Intelligence Agencies*—We have *16* agencies of the federal government concerned with intelligence. They sound like alphabet soup: CIA, NSA, DIA, NIS, NCS, and so on.

- *Congressional Subcommittees*—Too many to enumerate. Every time a new issue comes along, Congress establishes a new subcommittee, to the detriment of good government.

Is it any wonder we feel overwhelmed using the analytic approach to systems problems?

Furthermore, we must consider that the world of systems consists of circular entities (and feedback loops), in which multiple causality is integrally tied to multiple effects in an open and free-flowing environment. Clearly, analytic thinking cannot begin to comprehend, much less manage, the reality of such a world—*which just happens to be the real world we live in.*

At first glance, systems thinking may appear more complex and multilevel than analytic or reductionist thinking, but once we become familiar with its central concepts and framework, we find it helps us detect *the order in complexity* and is more accommodating to our understanding of reality. The conceptual linchpin of systems thinking, and of

Start thinking of systems as circular entities!

its mindset, is that *all systems are circular entities.* This concept, which is based on the actual nature of systems, is integral to the input-transformation-output-feedback model that forms the framework for systems thinking and reflects the natural order of life.

Once we get used to the systems thinking mindset, complexities fade away and our perspective is like that of an astronaut, someone taking a higher but no less accurate view of things . . . seeing the world as it really is, not as people wish it to be or assume it to be because of Machine Age ideas. Through the four elegantly simple concepts described next, anyone can adopt this mindset.

MOVING INTO THE SYSTEMS THINKING MINDSET

As we saw in the Introduction, the systems thinking mindset relies on the four concepts below. All are essential to our understanding of systems and systems change. We'll look at each one in turn.

1. The Seven Levels of Living (Open) Systems

In his classic book, *Living Systems*, James G. Miller contributed this key concept of systems levels, which is being used more frequently in today's organizations. The seven levels form a specific hierarchy of systems:

> ➡ **THE FOUR CONCEPTS OF SYSTEMS THINKING**
>
> 1. The Seven Levels of Living (Open) Systems
> 2. The Laws of Natural Systems: Standard Systems Dynamics
> 3. The A-B-C-D Systems Model
> 4. Changing Systems: The Natural Cycles of Life and Change

1. *Cell*—The basic unit of life

2. *Organ*—The organic systems within our bodies

3. *Organism*—Single organisms such as humans, animals, fish, birds

4. *Group*—Teams, departments, families, and similar bodies composed of members

5. *Organization*—Firm, company, neighborhood, community, city, private and public organizations, and nonprofit organizations

6. *Society*—States, provinces, countries, nations, regions within countries

7. *Supranational system*—Global systems, continents, regions, Earth

Our Focus in This Guidebook. We will be concerned primarily with the living systems at these three levels:

3. Organisms—Individuals
4. Group—Teams and departments
5. Organization—Companies, firms, communities

We will also focus on the intersections of these systems with one another; that is, the "collision" of systems with other systems. Those intersections are expressed as:

3A. One-to-one
4A. Between departments
5A. Organization and its environment

To conduct a systematic large-scale change effort, we must look at all three systems levels and all three collisions of levels. Also, we must be aware that the further we move towards the higher-level systems, the more complex the system will be—and the greater our need for the skills, willingness, and readiness to deal with that complexity. *See the learning aid on the following page for a depiction of the six levels as the Six Rings of Focus and Readiness.*

Systems Within Systems: Interrelationship. The systems hierarchy illustrates the interrelatedness and interdependence of systems, and the impact that systems have on one another. Thus does the hierarchy validate the concept of "systems within systems"—another key element to applying the lost art of systems thinking.

In viewing our organizations in this way—as *levels* of systems within, and colliding with, other systems—we align ourselves with the principles of openness, interrelation, and interdependence, and so cement the systems concept. When problem-solving, we look for *patterns of behavior and events,* rather than at isolated events, and we work on understanding how each *pattern* relates to the whole. We begin to see how problems are connected to *other* problems—and are forced to look at solving those problems in a new light. In fact, the solution to any systems problem is usually found at the next highest system (see the Einstein quotation in

LEARNING AID

CONCEPT I. THE SEVEN LEVELS OF LIVING (OPEN) SYSTEMS

HIERARCHY
1. Cell
2. Organ

3. Organism/Individual
4. Group/Team   Organizational
5. Organization   Focus
6. Society/Community

7. Supranational System

LEVELS OF THINKING

Problems that are created by our current level of thinking can't be solved by that same level of thinking.

—Albert Einstein

If we generally use analytic thinking, we now need real systems thinking to resolve our issues.

—Stephen G. Haines

The Six Rings of Focus and Readiness

3A. Organization-Environment

3. Total Organization
2A. Between Departments
2. Workteams
1A. One-to-One
1. Self

READINESS ➤ HIGH RINGS

Increased
– Complexity
– Readiness-Willingness
– Skills Growth

Note: *Rings 3, 4, 5 are three of the seven levels of living systems.*
Rings 3A, 4A, 5A are "collisions" of systems with other systems.

the learning aid). With this approach we end up with precisely what we need: fully integrated solutions to our systems problems.

2. The Laws of Natural Systems: Standard Systems Dynamics

Standard systems dynamics, found in all living systems, exhibit 12 characteristics, the focus of our discussion here. They have been adapted, with my own comments, from *Academy of Management Journal* (December, 1972), and organized into four categories as follows:

I. THE WHOLE
Characteristics:
1. *Holism (Synergism, Organicism, Gestalt)*
2. *Open Systems*
3. *System Boundaries*
4. *Input-Transformation-Output Model*
5. *Feedback*

II. THE GOALS
Characteristics:
6. *Multiple Outcomes / Goal-Seeking*
7. *Equifinality of Open Systems*

III. THE INTERNAL WORKINGS
Characteristics:
8. *Entropy*
9. *Hierarchy*
10. *Interrelated Parts (Subsystems or Components)*

IV. THE LONG-TERM RESULTS
Characteristics:
11. *Dynamic Equilibrium (Steady State)*
12. *Internal Elaboration*

Although it is important to understand each individual characteristic, keep in mind that it is the *relationship* between these *parts* and *characteristics,* and their *fit* into one *whole system,* that is key. Systems dynamics are all about relationships.

I. THE WHOLE

1. Holism (Synergism, Organicism, Gestalt). The whole is not just the sum of its parts; the system itself can be explained only as a totality. Holism is the opposite of elementarism, which views the total as the sum of its individual parts. For instance, we write letters, but our hands cannot write alone, as separate parts; they can only do so as part of our overall human system.

This leads us to the basic definition of a system as a holistic unit that is "the natural way of life." A system has overall purposes and transformational synergy when it is optimally effective.

➡ *Example*

Many managers believe a corporate strategic plan is just a "roll-up" of lower-level plans. This is a clear case of elementarism, one that usually results in poor implementation and that perpetuates a lot of turf battles and "silos." People lack holistic vision and a strategic plan to serve as an overall framework for efficiency and cooperation.

➡ *Experienced Dynamics*

Instead of holism, we usually see ineffective change that is parts- or activity-focused, leading to suboptimal results.

2. Open Systems. Systems are usually either (1) relatively closed, or (2) relatively open. As we saw earlier, open systems receive inputs from their environment, work with those inputs, and return them to the environment in modified form as outputs; in other words, open systems exchange information, energy, or material with their environment. Biological and social systems are inherently open systems; mechanical systems may be open or closed.

The three keys to success for any system are its ability (1) to be interactive with its environment, (2) to fit that environment, and (3) to be connected to that environment. A crucial task for any system is to scan the environment and then adapt to it.

➡ *Example*

Excellent organizations are marked by their intense desire to be open to feedback and their constant search for information from their environment that will help them thrive and lead.

➡ *Experienced Dynamics*

Many organizations and their cultures are relatively closed systems with a low environmental scan—a myopic view in today's rapidly changing world.

3. Systems Boundaries. When we consider the above, it naturally follows that all systems have boundaries which separate them from their environments. The concept of boundaries furthers our understanding of the distinction between open and closed systems. The relatively closed system has rigid, impenetrable boundaries, whereas the open system has permeable boundaries between itself and a broader suprasystem. Thus an open system can more easily integrate and collaborate with its environment.

Boundaries are no trouble to define in physical and biological systems, but they are quite difficult to delineate in social systems, such as communities and organizations.

This may be why our legislative systems provide so much protection for individual rights, and less for "the common good" of a community.

In organizations, the boundaries are relatively open, which makes them somewhat vague in terms of our knowing and fully understanding their limits. In today's society, with its worldwide, instantaneous communications, our boundaries are increasingly more open.

➡ *Example*

To shift from analytic to systems thinking, we must be able to recognize systems and their boundaries; only then can we work with, and hope to change, the system.

➡ *Experienced Dynamics*

We often see closed boundaries leading to fragmentation, turf battles, separation, and parochialism, when integration and collaboration is what is needed.

4. Input-Transformation-Output Model. The open system can be viewed as a transformation model. Its relationship with its environment is dynamic: it receives various inputs, transforms these inputs in some way, and exports outputs. This is the way natural and living systems operate—and *the core systems thinking model and framework* that you must internalize if you want to use systems thinking in a practical way. The model can be combined with Feedback (characteristic 5) and the Seven Levels of Systems Thinking (systems concept 1) to create a flow chart showing how systems change and transform over time.

➡ *Example*

On the most basic level, we must take inputs (e.g., food and water) and transform them into vital nutrients if we are to survive rather than perish.

➡ *Experienced Dynamics*

Because our piecemeal analytic and reductionist view of the world is so narrow, we often miss outcomes—feedback and environmental considerations.

5. Feedback. This is important to our understanding of how a system maintains a steady state. Information concerning the system's outputs or process is fed back into the system as an input, perhaps leading to changes in the transformation process to achieve more effective future outputs. Often this informational input helps us get to the root of problems.

Feedback can be either positive or negative. Positive feedback indicates that the steady state of a system is presently effective. Negative feedback indicates that the system is deviating from a prescribed course and should readjust to a new steady state. Some systems-related field, such as cybernetics, are based on negative feedback.

Both forms of feedback stimulate learning and change. It is essential for us to receive and understand feedback, even (and very often *especially*) when the news is bad and suggests root causes and underlying problems we'd rather not hear about.

➡ *Example*

The basic concept of the learning organization, as distinct from all the rhetoric surrounding it, directs us toward gathering as much feedback as possible, even negative feedback, so we can act on it to create new learning. Only through feedback can organizations hope to learn and grow at all systems levels—individual, team, and organization.

➡ *Experienced Dynamics*

We often get very little informational input about our performance or the performance of the organization itself. What we tend to get is financial feedback—only part of the overall picture.

II. THE GOALS

6. Multiple Outcomes/Goal-Seeking. Biological and social systems appear to have multiple goals or purposes. Social organizations set multiple goals, if for no other reason than that their members and subunits have different values and objectives. Goal achievement in today's multi-cultural, diverse society is particularly difficult, for we as members of that society bring such an assortment of goals to it.

Since this is a characteristic of all systems, it follows that a common, detailed vision for any organization or society is crucial to coordinated and focused actions by its members.

➡ *Example*
The clash between individual and organizational goals in present-day organizations causes much conflict and lost productivity for all concerned, ultimately creating lose-lose situations. It has contributed to the dehumanization, delayering, and mechanization of work, alienating many of today's workers.

➡ *Experienced Dynamics*
Often, instead of embracing multiple outcomes, we engage in *artificial either/or thinking*, which leads to conflict rather than cooperation.

7. Equifinality of Open Systems. In mechanistic systems there is a direct cause-and-effect relationship between the initial conditions and the final state. Biological and social systems operate differently. Equifinality suggests that certain results may be achieved with different initial conditions and in different ways. It offers us a basis for the flexibility, agility, and choice needed in today's dynamic world.

This view suggests that social organizations can accomplish their objectives with diverse inputs and with varying internal activities (processes). For this reason, there is usually not one "best" way to solve most problems; in other words, as the saying goes, there's more than one way to skin a cat!

➡ *Example*

Because we lack one "best" way to solve organizational problems, it is crucial for us to be "strategically consist-ent" to consensual, multiple goals, yet "operationally flexible" (or empowering) in working to achieve those goals. This encourages us to challenge our minds—to employ our mental skills in determining *how* to achieve goals. And as long as our goals are clear and based on a shared vision, we can succeed at it.

➡ *Experienced Dynamics*

Too often we ignore the complexity of an issue, insist-ing upon, and fighting about, the "best way to do things." We immediately look for a direct, one-to-one, cause-and-effect relationship that would explain the issue; then we try to find a simple, singular solution. But such solutions *do not* work in a systems world, that is, our world today.

III. THE INTERNAL WORKINGS

8. Entropy. Physical systems are subject to the force of entropy, which increases until eventually the entire system fails. The tendency toward maximum entropy is a move-ment to disorder, complete lack of resource transformation, and death. For instance, people with anorexia do not consume enough food to maintain their physical bodies; if the disorder continues, they perish.

In a closed system, the change in entropy must always be "positive," meaning toward death. However, in open biological or social systems, entropy can be arrested and may even be transformed into negative entropy—a process of more complete organization and enhanced ability to transform resources. Why? Because the system imports energy and resources from its environment, leading to renewal. This is why education and learning are so important, as they provide new and stimulating input (termed *neg-entropy*) that can transform each of us.

"From the time we're born, we begin to die" is an apt adage here. Our cells completely regenerate every seven years through neg-entropy, and, in a sense, we become completely new persons. Regular follow-up and feedback are key to this needed renewal.

➡ *Example*

Most change efforts fail because they aren't given enough follow-up, reinforcement, and new energy. Many managers want to get everything up and running on autopilot, but this is the antithesis of what actually makes change happen. In systems terms, it takes negative entropy—new energy—to make change occur. In fact, most executives are concerned about getting employee "buy-in," when "stay-in" is even more difficult to get and retain over time (for more on this topic, see Haines, *Sustaining High Performance*).

➡ *Experienced Dynamics*

Lack of negative entropy, or new energy, is what leads to obsolescence, rigidity, decline, and (ultimately) death.

9. Hierarchy. A system consists of subsystems (lower-order systems) and is itself part of a suprasystem (higher-order system). Any living system thus has a hierarchy of components. In today's politically correct environment, the concept of hierarchy is quite unpopular, but it is a permanent fact of life. The issue is to "flatten" the hierarchy as much as possible—to "go with the flow" of life and what makes sense, in a natural, self-organizing type of way. What we do not want is the imposition of rigid and artificial structures.

Since systems are hierarchical, the organizational system is higher than the department/unit/team as a system, which is higher than the individual employee as a system (whether we're happy about that or not). If we don't like the hierarchy or fit, we need to work either to change how the hierarchy operates, or to lessen it; however, it cannot be eliminated, as some would naively propose—it's simply inherent in systems.

➡ *Example*

To get an idea of how hierarchies work in the natural world, and how essential they are to it, think about the food chain—an inescapable hierarchy, found in both terrestrial and aquatic environments, and often crossing between them.

➡ *Experienced Dynamics*

Instead of finding natural, common-sensical hierarchies in our organizations, we often find artificial, rigid hierarchies; they are usually subject to bloated bureaucracies based on the old "command and control," as if we can ever truly and surely control others.

10. Interrelated Parts (Subsystems or Components).
By definition, a system is composed of interrelated parts or elements in some kind of relationship with one another.

This is true for all systems— mechanical, biological, and social. Every system has at least two elements, and these elements are interconnected.

The whole idea of a system is to optimize—*not* maximize— the fit of its elements in order to maximize the whole. If we merely maximize the elements of systems, we end up sub-optimizing the whole (2 plus 2 equals 3—less than it should, and less than we want it to).

To get a handle on this concept, consider what happens to college football players who try to artificially maximize their muscles and weight with steroids: they do serious long-term harm to their bodies, and sometimes the damage is so severe it leads to premature death.

➡ *Example*

In organizations, it is vital to get all the related sub-systems working together toward the achievement of business goals. However, too often departments compete with one another, individually attempting to maximize their influence in the organization, to the detriment of other departments and, ultimately, to that of the organization as a whole.

Balancing the demands of each department is difficult and should be a key role of senior organizational leaders. Unfortunately, this leads to conflict-resolution issues and skills that many leaders in both private and public organizations would rather ignore.

➡ *Experienced Dynamics*

We often experience artificial and separate silos, parts and components that managers try mightily to protect; but doing so is impossible in a system with natural and related parts.

IV. THE LONG-TERM RESULTS

11. Dynamic Equilibrium (Steady State). The concept of a dynamic equilibrium in "steady state" is closely related to that of negative entropy. A closed system eventually must attain an equilibrium state with maximum entropy: death or disorganization. However, an open system may attain a state whereby the system remains in dynamic equilibrium through the continuous inflow of materials, energy, information, and feedback. This leads to balance and stability. Unfortunately, it also feeds resistance to change, creating "ruts" and habits.

Our tendency to resist change in our lives and in our organizations, and to return to balance through dynamic equilibrium, is normal and natural. However, in today's rapidly changing environment, if we want the stability we desire, we must become adaptable and flexible to change in a personal way.

➡ *Example*

Dynamic equilibrium is why culture change in organizations is far more difficult to achieve than isolated change. Culture change requires modifying *all* aspects of the organization's internal workings so the whole will enter a new "steady state."

➡ *Experienced Dynamics*

Resistance to change often leads to short-term myopic views and actions that lead nowhere.

12. Internal Elaboration. Closed systems move toward entropy and disorganization. In contrast, open systems tend to move toward greater differentiation, elaboration, and detail, and a higher level of organizational sophistication. This may sound good, but it can actually lead to organizational complexity and bureaucracy in its worst form. Complexity must be continuously resisted, for it develops naturally; it is also part of the natural process of ossification, rigidity, and death.

➡ *Example*

This is why the KISS method and the directives to clarify and simplify are so crucial to success in our lives and organizations. Also, the "elimination of waste," in total quality management and reengineering terms, is a positive trend toward reversing ossification.

➡ *Experienced Dynamics*

Organizational growth, with all its complexities, often leads us into confusion or outright chaos; we're at a loss for ideas that can help us manage such a situation. Systems thinking changes all that.

☞ *Be sure to see the learning aid for standard systems dynamics, on the following page.*

---

3. The A-B-C-D Systems Model

Do you usually think in terms of outputs, feedback, inputs, and throughputs, and how they relate to their environment? If not, don't feel bad—you're not alone. All of them are phases of the A-B-C-D Systems Model, a conceptual framework that gives systems thinkers an effective way to view systems. Its name is a reflection of our definition of a system:

> *A set of components that work together for the good of the whole*

This point underscores how essential the model is to our adopting the systems thinking mindset.

LEARNING AID

CONCEPT 2. THE LAWS OF NATURAL SYSTEMS: STANDARD SYSTEMS DYNAMICS

Natural Laws/Desired State vs. Experienced Dynamics

Natural Laws/Desired State	Experienced Dynamics
1. **Holism:** Overall purpose—focused synergy; transformation	1. Parts- and activity-focused; suboptimal results
2. **Open Systems:** Open to environment	2. Closed systems; low environmental scan
3. **Boundaries:** Integrated; collaborative integrated; collaborative	3. Fragmented; turf battles; separate; parochial
4. **Input/Output:** How natural systems operate	4. Piecemeal and narrow analytic view of world
5. **Feedback:** On effectiveness; on root causes of problems	5. Low feedback; financial feedback only
6. **Multiple Outcomes:** Goals	6. Artificial either/or thinking
7. **Equifinality:** Flexibility and agility	7. Direct cause-and-effect; one "best" way
8. **Entropy:** Follow-up; inputs of energy; renewal	8. Decline; rigidity; obsolescence; death
9. **Hierarchy:** Flatter organization; self-organizing	9. Hierarchy; bureaucracy; command and control
10. **Interrelated Parts:** Relationships; participation	10. Separate parts, components, entities; silos
11. **Dynamic Equilibrium:** Culture; stability and balance	11. Short-term myopic view; ruts; resistance to change
12. **Internal Elaboration:** Details and sophistication	12. Complexity and confusion

FIGURE 1. Conceptual Model

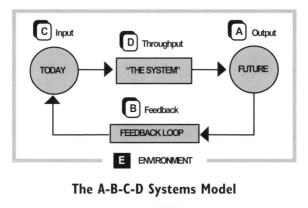

The A-B-C-D Systems Model

Understanding and Using the Model. To comprehend our model (shown in Figure 1), we first must understand that a system is anything but a static entity; rather, it is a living, ongoing process that requires inputs, outputs, and feedback. The activities associated with these requirements constitute the various phases of the process.

In terms of looking at those phases in order to effect change in a system, we must begin where analytic thinking would have us end up—at the output phase. We ask "Where do we want to be?" and then think and work backwards through the system phases to create the desired future state (this is partly why some people refer to systems thinking as "backwards thinking").

When applied to problem solving, the model focuses us on results (outputs) rather than knee-jerk solutions, and so we work toward better, longer-term answers and solutions. When everyone in an organization knows how to frame issues in this way, discussions about problems (and group problem-solving efforts in general) take on a new dimension—one in which clarity and focus are possible, despite all the complexity. Thus it is important to teach the model to organizational members at all levels.

FIGURE 2. Alternative View of the A-B-C-D Systems Model

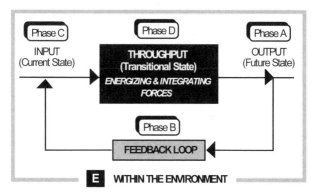

Figure 2 further elucidates the systems thinking framework. It details the states that correspond to the A, C, and D phases, particularly that of the Phase D, Throughput. You may find this a handy addition when teaching the model to others.

The Phases of the A-B-C-D Systems Model. Each model phase leads us to a particular question that guides our thinking and problem-solving. It is essential to remember that, in asking any question, we keep in mind a fifth, ongoing question: *What is changing in the environment that we need to consider?* Now let's take a closer look.

PHASE A—OUTPUT. This is the defining phase in the systems model, the output that results from the system's activity. It leads us to the crucial question:

> ➤ *Where do we want to be?*
> (What are our outcomes? purposes? goals?)

This is the Number One question that systems thinkers ask when they are dealing with any situation or problem. It should always be asked in the context of the system's environment and other system levels.

PHASE B—FEEDBACK LOOP. It is at this point in systems thinking that we start thinking backward to determine what must take place for our desired outcome to occur. We ask:

> ➤ *How will we know we have reached it?*
> (How will we know we have achieved the outcomes, purposes, or goals?)

Phase B is where we decide how we will measure our achievement. We then feed that decision back into the system. This phase also operates as a way to see if Phase A needs more work; for example, we may find the goal has been too broadly defined and needs redefinition.

> ☞ Be sure to keep asking the question . . .
> *What is changing in the environment that we need to consider?*

PHASE C—INPUT. In this phase we begin to create strategies for closing the gap between what is happening right now and what should happen in the future. We ask the question:

> ➤ **Where are we right now?**
> (What are today's issues and problems?)

Analytic thinkers *start* with today's issues; so they end up problem-solving isolated events. Instead, we must see today's issues in light of desired outcomes.

PHASE D—THROUGHPUT. Now we look at the system and its interdependencies, and ask:

> ➤ **How do we get from here to our desired place?**
> (How do we close the gap from A to C in a complete, holistic way?)

With those interdependencies in mind, we focus on the processes, activities, and relationships that the system must implement in order to produce the desired outcome. We also plan for the processes that must be developed and put into motion now.

The Unlimited Uses of the Systems Model. Any set of requirements can be adapted to the model as long as you use the same A-B-C-D locator phases and include the environment. Some of the model's many organizational applications are included in later chapters; however, as a framework and an orientation to life, the model is applicable to virtually *any* situation you encounter. Use it in all that you think about, act upon, and evaluate.

LEARNING AID

Concept 3. The A-B-C-D Systems Model

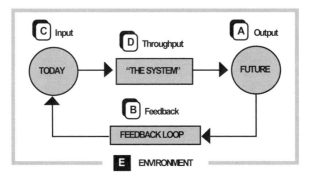

THE SYSTEMS-PHASE QUESTIONS, IN SEQUENCE

A. **Where do we want to be?** (What are our outcomes, purposes, goals?)

B **How will we know we have reached it?** (How will we know we have achieved the outcomes, purposes, goals?)

C. **Where are we now?** (What are today's issues and problems?)

D. **How do we get from here to our desired place? (**How do we close the gap from C to A in a complete, holistic way?)

ALSO: What is changing in the environment that we need to consider? (This is an ongoing question throughout all phases.)

WHY THINKING MATTERS *How you think is how you act is how you are.*	The way you think creates the results you get. The most powerful way to improve the quality of your results is to improve the way you think.

4. Changing Systems: The Natural Cycles of Life and Change

Our natural world does not operate in a linear, sequential fashion, despite all our training and traditional models. Life expresses itself in cycles of change, such as the turn of generations and the seasonal year. Even the bull and bear markets on Wall Street aren't immune to such cycles. I call this natural rhythm of life *the Rollercoaster of Change,* a name that takes into account the complexities of change in our dynamic world.

The following are a few historical and natural cycles of change and learning.

The Environment	Civilizations	Historical Ages
• Ocean tides • Volcanoes • Whale & bird migration • Lunar cycle • Day & night	• Inca, Aztec, Mayan empires • Chinese dynasties • Roman Empire • British Empire	• Hunting & gathering • Dark Ages • Agricultural • Industrial • Information Age
Industries	**Travel**	**Life**
• Start-Up • High-Growth • Maturity • Decline • Renewal	• Automobile • Ocean liner • Mass Transit • Airplanes • Space shuttle	• Birth, death, new generation • Food chain • Food cycle • Growth, decline

We as human, living systems keep on changing. It is a natural part of life (and death). Change is constant. The key is *finding simplicity on the far side of complexity*. The Rollercoaster of Change, presented in the following learning aid, helps us get there. Its many uses will be discussed later, in a variety of tools.

LEARNING AID

Concept 4. Changing Systems: The Natural Cycles of Life and Change

"The Rollercoaster of Change"
(The Key to Strategic Change)

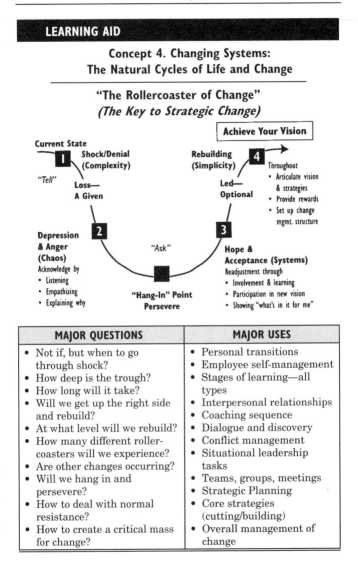

MAJOR QUESTIONS	MAJOR USES
• Not if, but when to go through shock?	• Personal transitions
• How deep is the trough?	• Employee self-management
• How long will it take?	• Stages of learning—all types
• Will we get up the right side and rebuild?	• Interpersonal relationships
• At what level will we rebuild?	• Coaching sequence
• How many different roller-coasters will we experience?	• Dialogue and discovery
• Are other changes occurring?	• Conflict management
• Will we hang in and persevere?	• Situational leadership tasks
• How to deal with normal resistance?	• Teams, groups, meetings
• How to create a critical mass for change?	• Strategic Planning
	• Core strategies (cutting/building)
	• Overall management of change

II. Standard Systems Dynamics

This chapter presents 12 tools that will help you apply the principles of standard systems dynamics and other key concepts to systems-related change efforts. The tools focus on the questions that good systems thinkers know and regularly use, and offer guidelines for working productively with the answers.

TOOL NO.	THE APPLICATIONS
1.	**Systems Preconditions** —*What entity (system or "collision of systems") are we dealing with, and what are its boundaries?* —*What levels of the overall entity do we want to change?*
2.	**Desired Outcomes** —*What are the desired outcomes?*
3.	**The Need for Feedback** —*How will we know we have achieved the desired outcomes?*
4.	**Environmental Impact** —*What is changing in the environment that we need to consider?*
5.	**Looking at Relationships** —*What is the relationship of x to y and z?*

(Continued)

TOOL NO.	THE APPLICATIONS *(Concluded)*
6.	**The What and the How** *—Are we dealing with ends (the what) or with means (the how)?*
7.	**The Iceberg Theory of Change** *—What new processes and structures are we using to ensure succesful change?*
8.	**Buy-In and Stay-In** *—What must we do to ensure buy-in and stay-in (perseverance) over time, and thus avoid the problem of entropy?*
9.	**Centralize and Decentralize** *—What should we centralize and what should we decentralize?*
10.	**Multiple Causes: Root Causes** *—What multiple causes lie at the root of our problem or concern? (That is, what are the root causes of our problem or concern?)*
11.	**KISS: From Complexity to Simplicity** *—How can we move from complexity to simplicity, and from strict consistency to flexibility, in the solutions we devise?*
12.	**The Ultimate Question: Superordinate Goals** *—What is our common higher-level (superordinate) goal?*
➡ **These Tools Will Get You Started on Systems Thinking!**	

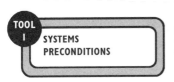

Application of
• Seven Levels of Living Systems
• Standard Systems Dynamics
  — 3. Boundaries

A. THE OBJECT OF CHANGE

To begin with, you must be clear on what overall system you are trying to change. You must also be clear on its boundaries, both physical and mental. Where does it all start and end? Your preliminary question is therefore:

 What entity (system or "collision of systems") are we dealing with, and what are its boundaries?

This question may seem obvious, but many people fail to ask it at all. They launch into change efforts with only a vague idea of what they want to change, and so quickly run into problems. Consider this question a *precondition* to any intelligent, effective action and change.

> ▶ **PRINCIPLE:** The entity to be changed must be clear.

Challenge the obvious—look for the seven levels of living systems and define which ones you are dealing with. Know the entity you want to change, and its limits.

➡ Example

Are you trying to change yourself, your department, a business process, a partnership, or the entire organization? Is it relatively open or closed in its environmental interactions?

Set realistic goals, focusing on what is actually achievable, even if with a stretch. "Think globally, act locally" is an apt phrase here.

1. Be clear on the entity you are discussing, especially its boundaries with the environment.

2. Be aware that solutions to issues of change and leadership will be different for each system level you deal with (see tool below). For instance, personal change and learning solutions are different from team or organizational change solutions.

3. Troubleshoot all solutions to predict their effects as best as possible. Will they help you achieve the desired changes in your entity of choice?

B. LEVELS OF CHANGE

To direct your change efforts accurately, you need to look closely at the entity's internal levels or "rings" and answer this question:

? *What levels of the overall entity do we want to change?*

In this section of Tool 1, we will focus on change that creates a high-performance organization. Such a goal requires that you pay attention to all the systems levels within the organization, and to the interactions of those systems—their "collision" with one another. Each level has unique purposes and solutions, and each is important to success.

Figure 3, on the next page, presents the "tree rings" of an overall organizational system. Note the recognition of the relationship between the rings (or levels). This kind of framing device can be used to depict the levels of any overall system.

FIGURE 3. STRATEGIC CHANGE

3A. Organization-Environment

3. Total Organization
2A. Between Departments
2. Workteams
1A. One-to-One
1. Self

READINESS → **HIGH RINGS**

Increased
– Complexity
– Readiness-Willingness
– Skills Growth

The Six Rings of Focus and Readiness

The General Objectives of Working at Each Level/Ring

Each system level corresponds to certain general improvement issues. For instance, if you goal is to improve personal competency, you will need to work primarily at the Self level/ring and take into consideration any other rings that have a bearing on competency matters.

The rings and their related issues are as follows:

1. **Self**—Individuals, self-mastery
    • Improve personal competency and effectiveness
    • Trustworthiness issues

1A. **One-to-One Relationships**—Interpersonal skills and effectiveness
    • Improve the interpersonal and working relationships and productivity of each individual
    • Trust issues

2. **Workteams**—Groups, team effectiveness
    • Improve the productivity of the team as well as its members
    • Empowerment and interpersonal roles and issues

2A. **Between Departments**—Intergroups, conflict/horizontal cooperation
- Improve the working relationships and business processes between teams/departments horizontally to serve the customer better
- Horizontal collaboration/integration issues (Note: This is the ring most likely to need improvements.)

3. **Total Organization**—The "fit"
- Improve the organization's systems, structures, and processes to better achieve business goals and develop potential; while pursuing your vision and strategic plan, develop the organization's capacity to provide an adaptive system of change
- Alignment issues

3A. **Organization-Environment**—Strategic plans
- Improve the organization's sense of direction, response to its customers, and proactive management of its environment and stakeholders by reinventing strategic planning for the demands of the future
- Adaptation to environmental issues

Organizational Change by Levels/Rings

The managers of the organization's levels/rings must get involved in the change. Each one should be given time to understand, accept, and integrate the change; consequently, the manager will own the vision and change and lead them at his or her level. Specific levels would include (in descending order of hierarchy):

- Board
- CEO
- Senior management (interpersonal relations)
- Middle management (department by department)
- Cross-functional (department by department) conflict resolution and cooperation
- Workers across entire organization

It is important to sell and resell the change throughout many organizational levels. Themes from the Rollercoaster of Change are useful in helping people come to terms with change. Notable among those themes are the following:

1. Awareness, shock, depression
2. Education, skills
3. Experimentation
4. Understanding, hope
5. Commitment to building the new vision
6. Fuller appreciation
7. Integration of ongoing behaviors

GUIDELINES FOR USE

I. Engineer success up front by determining which rings of the organization you are trying to change. Also, determine what other rings will need changing first in order for you to achieve your desired outcome.

2. Always be sure to look at the purposes of the rings you are trying to change. Begin by using the list of purposes presented in this tool; then think of purposes unique to your situation.

3. Get people involved in the change effort, particularly managers. Remember: you don't just want buy-in from managers; you also want stay-in from them.

   Also, be sure to look at *all* the rings of your organization. As you have seen in this tool, that means board members and CEOs too!

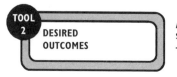

TOOL 2 — DESIRED OUTCOMES

Application of
Standard Systems Dynamics
— 6. Multiple Outcomes

Success

The great successful men (and women) of the world have used their imagination. . . . They think ahead and create their mental picture, and then go to work materializing that picture in all its details, filling in here, adding a little there, altering this a bit and that a bit, but steadily building— steadily building.

—Robert Collier

This is where Phase A of the A-B-C-D Systems Model actually begins, and so we ask the Number One system's thinking question:

> **?** **What are the desired outcomes? (That is, Where do we want to be?)**

Since systems usually have multiple outcomes, this is a more complex question than it appears at first glance.

> **➤ PRINCIPLE: Systems are goal-seeking.**

Develop clarity and agreement on this before starting to act. Keep in mind there are usually multiple outcomes (we're not dealing with either/or questions as reductionist thinkers do). Other words for outcomes (the "what") include *vision, ends, goals, objectives, mission, purpose.*

Without agreement on ends, our actions will never have a chance of succeeding. Once the "what" is clear, there are many ways to try to attain it, such as by empowerment.

➡ **For Example**

Organizational outcomes often include the needs of
customers, employees, and stockholders, as well as
the community, suppliers, and so forth. Asking this
question sends us into "backwards thinking," which
keeps us from focusing on only isolated events.

Further, these desired outcomes are all about setting
goals. Goal setting and careful goal selection (that is, the
establishment of a vision or purpose and meaning) are
primary criteria for success.

➡ **For Example**

In simple, meetings-management terms, it means
making daily "to do" lists like the one below, so you
focus on actions and results, not just quick talk and
a few good ideas.

Meetings "To Do" List

What to Do/Achieve	By Whom	By When

GUIDELINES FOR USE

I.   Make this tool's question your Number One question too.
     Ask it before you do anything in life, whether what you
     do is work-related or not. Remember, this is synonymous
     with Phase A's question:

Where do we want to be?

TOOL 3 — THE NEED FOR FEEDBACK

Application of
Standard Systems Dynamics
— 5. Feedback

Once we have identified our desired outcomes, we need to address the all-important question:

 How will we know we have achieved the desired outcomes?

This corresponds to the A-B-C-D System Model's Phase B question, *How will we know we have reached it (the place we want to be)?*

The concept of feedback is important to our understanding of how a system maintains a steady state or changes successfully. In practical terms, information concerning the system's outputs is fed back into the system as an input— that is, the results of past performance are reinserted into the system—and if need be, the system's behavior is modified. *Positive* feedback tells us the system is "on course" to achieving the desired outcomes; *negative* feedback indicates the system is "off course" and must change. Negative feedback is actually good in the sense that it stimulates learning. In fact, the ability to manage such feedback well is a survival skill today.

> ▶ **PRINCIPLE:** As an input, feedback requires receptivity; it calls for us to be flexible and adaptable.

Because our world is so changeable, solutions that work today may simply not work tomorrow; therefore, despite the importance of finding initial solutions to problems, our primary concern is to ensure we receive constant feedback and know how to work with it. The ability to be flexible and adaptable is crucial here; fortunately, the more we receive and work with feedback, the better our ability becomes. Feedback teaches us to learn, grow, adapt, and change as our goals and environment require. It is a vital input of learning organizations, helping people at all system levels (individual, team, and organization) deal with change personally and professionally.

GUIDELINES FOR USE

1. Look at feedback as a gift—be open and receptive to it; even encourage it. Ask for feedback from all your customers, your employees, your direct reports and peers, and anyone who can help you learn and grow as a person, as a professional, as a leader of your organization.

2. Work on developing self-mastery—the interpersonal style needed to genuinely encourage others to provide feedback, and the mental attitude needed to stay receptive even when feedback is negative. Don't be defensive, and always thank the feedback giver. Remember, you're the one who decides, after some reflection, whether the feedback merits action and, if so, what action to take.

3. Ensure that feedback in your organization is received and applied in the context of the entire system. Limiting feedback to select levels is like limiting team-performance results to select team members: it makes no sense at all, especially if changes are needed.

4. Bring to your organization all that you personally learn about feedback, receptivity, flexibility, and adaptability. The more senior your level in the organization, the more important this is.

TOOL 4 — ENVIRONMENTAL IMPACT

Application of
Standard Systems Dynamics
— 2. Open Systems
— 3. Boundaries

Organizations and individuals who do not constantly scan their environment to see what is changing are unlikely to be successful in today's world. Therefore, we must continually ask:

 What is changing in the environment that we we need to consider?

In organizational terms, this means we must keep scanning the environment for changes in anything from our competition to the political scene. At minimum there are seven areas we need to keep an eye on. They can be remembered by the acronym SKEPTIC.

Socio-demographics	**T**echnology
"**K**"ompetition	**I**ndustry
Economics	**C**ustomers
Politics	

In terms of the individual, it means paying attention to environmental changes that may have an impact on our roles in life. We should consider at least four areas, which we can remember by the acronym PITO.

Personal—Body, mind, spirit
Interpersonal—Family, friends, colleagues
Team—Associations, community, department
Organization—Job, career, wealth

> ➤ **PRINCIPLE:** Systems require work and alignment from the outside in, not the inside out.

Remember to employ "backwards thinking." Start with the environment—the wants and needs of the customer, for example—and the desired outcomes; then work backwards into the organization to determine how to meet the demands of the environment, and the outcomes, while still meeting the multiple needs of other key stakeholders in the environment.

Align all employees, suppliers, the entire organization, and business processes across departments to meet those demands and produce the desired outcomes. This is the conceptual basis for business process reengineering in today's organizations. However, it is often fragmented into departmental elements or internal cost-cutting activities, and it neglects to consider customer impact.

GUIDELINES FOR USE

1. Set up an environmental scanning system in your organization, and assign a senior person or team the responsibility of collecting data on each SKEPTIC area.

2. Conduct quarterly environmental scanning sessions in which everyone shares information they have gathered. From this, deduce trends and impacts on your organization.

3. Annually revise your strategic plan, with the above as key input.

4. Keep yourself open to what is changing in the environment. Find out what is going on not just through the typical media, such as television and newspapers, but through other means as well, such newsletters.

TOOL 5
LOOKING AT RELATIONSHIPS

Application of
• Seven Levels of Living Systems
• Standard Systems Dynamics
— 9. Hierarchy
—10. Interrelated Parts

A. THE QUESTION OF RELATIONSHIP

In systems thinking, we are always looking at the relationship of the part or event to both (1) the overall system outcomes, and (2) all other parts and events within the system. We ask the question:

 What is the relationship of x to y and z?

To fully address the question, we must keep in mind:

• In systems, the whole is primary and the parts/events are secondary. The parts are only important within their relationship to other parts/events.
• Balance and optimization is the key, not dominance and maximization of a single part.
• In systems, relationships and processes are what's important; not departments/units and events.
• We need to think from events and parts to relationships and processes.

> ▶ **PRINCIPLE:** The whole is more important that the part; relationships and processes are key.

It is essential for us to continually assess how the parts fit or link together in an integrated process in support of the whole outcome. Moreover, each part's effectiveness cannot be analyzed in a void, but only in relationship to the other parts and the processes that lead to the whole. Always remember, a system cannot be subdivided into independent parts. Change in one part affects the whole and the other interdependent parts or processes. This is true whether we are talking about teams, departments, and organizations, or society as a whole—something we all still need to learn and understand.

➡ For Example

In organizations, the question is not, How can I maximize my job or department's impact?; it is, How can we all work and fit together in support of the overall objectives of the organization? To that end, each year all major departments need to share their annual plans with senior executives and middle managers and other professionals to ensure everyone knows what everyone else is doing, and to give others a chance to critique those plans. This is actually a large group team-building process.

In personal terms, systems thinking is about finding patterns and relationships in your work and your life, and learning to reinforce or change these patterns to achieve personal fulfillment. This can actually help simplify your life, as you see interconnections between what initially seem like disperate parts.

➡ For Example

What is the relationship between your fitness and energy level, your overall feeling of health, and the stamina needed to do your job and run your life each day? In looking at a question like this, you begin to apply system thinking to your life.

Create *synergy* in your life. Synergy is the working together of two or more parts of any system, to produce an effect greater than the sum of the parts' individual effects. It is increasing your outcomes by working with others in a particularly effective way.

GUIDELINES FOR USE

1. In using this tool, remember the principle of interdependence. We have only to look at photographs of Earth to know that all of us are parts of the same global fabric, with patterns of interdependency linking us. Apply this kind of vision to your life and to your organization.

2. Focus on your interrelatedness with others in your life, and think about how your visions (intents and desired outcomes) affect others. Share these visions, asking for feedback on them on a regular basis. Pay attention to your impact on others, and think about their impact on you. Keep asking the question *What is the relationship of x to y and z?*

3. On a professional level, get others thinking about interdependencies and interrelationships between systems levels and parts. Propose this tool's question as a basis for thought when problem solving.

B. COROLLARY: SOLVING THE EITHER/OR PUZZLE

A puzzle is a problem that we usually cannot solve because we make an incorrect assumption or self-imposed constraint that precludes solution.

—Russ Ackoff (1991)

The analytic tyranny of either/or questions dictates that we must select one of two options (x or y), and *only* one; thus it sets up an immediate opposition between two things (x versus y), often at the expense of our seeing connections and interrelationships that could lead to better problem solving.

Furthermore, many issues have multiple causes and multiple outcomes, and by looking at them in an either/or fashion, we fail to see the entire picture. If we want to avoid this pitfall, and similar pitfalls related to this-versus-that thinking, then we need to defy the analytic tyranny by answering either/or questions with an emphatic *"Yes, both."*

The one "best" answer must evolve into the answers we need to truly solve the problems that confront us. That requires us to stress the "and" of things—to develop the ability to embrace, at any one time, *two or more different opinions, extremes, or seemingly contradictory statements.* This is the genius of systems thinking. Instead of turning problems into puzzles, it looks at them head-on.

➡ **For Example**

The question "Is it *x* or *y*?" is usually based on an incorrect assumption: that there is only one answer in all cases. This mistaken assumption occurs in organizations, in families, in all interpersonal relationships, and often results in needless conflict, differences of opinions, and hard feelings.

GUIDELINES FOR USE

1. Don't get caught up in either/or debates. State areas of agreement first, rather than debating; then state your area of disagreement *if* there actually is one. When someone asks you an either/or question, answer "Yes, both" to surface artificial disagreement.

2. Learn to distinguish between the tyranny of either/or questions and the more open process of making distinctions between things. (If someone held up a pencil and asked, "Is this a pencil or a pen," you would not say "Yes, both.")

3. Get others in your organization thinking in less oppositional ways. A close look at either/or questions is a good way to start people thinking about assumptions in general and the danger of unexamined ones.

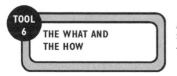

TOOL
6
THE WHAT AND
THE HOW

Application of
Standard Systems Dynamics
— 4. Input-Output

A. ENDS AND MEANS

To work effectively toward the desired outcomes, and to communicate clearly about them, we must distinguish between the ends (the what) and the means (the how) at our system level. We should ask:

 Are we dealing with the ends (the what) or with the means (the how)?

Here are our definitions of these terms:

The Ends (The What):   The multiple outcomes
The Means (The How):   The many different ways to achieve
                        the same outcomes; process, fit and
                        interrelationship of parts are key.

Their relation to the A-B-C-D Systems Model is shown below, along with inputs and specific examples.

Phase C = Inputs ➡ Phase D = Means/How ➡ Phase A = Ends/What		
(Input Phase)	(Throughput Phase)	(Output Phase)
• Strategies	• Tasks, activities, actions	• Goals, results, objectives
• Resources	• Processes, operations,	• Vision, mission, values
• Information, data	departments	• Outcomes, purposes
• People, money facilities	• Elements, parts, components	

It is important to realize that *what constitutes an outcome to you and your systems level is a means to an end for the larger system.* The what of one person (or department or team) is therefore a how of the larger organization—and the systems hierarchy within the overall system is *the* how (along with input from the organization's environment). All levels need to understand what the ends of the overall system are, or confusion can set in.

➡ **For Example**

Large-company divisions often do not know the multiple outcomes of the overall system. This is why such divisions tend to be perplexed by "higher-up" decisions.

> ➤ **PRINCIPLE:** All systems are linked to other systems (some larger, some smaller) in the hierarchy.

No system is independent of any other; we are all linked together in hierarchies of systems. Pay attention to the sets of linkages within the organization system and between the organization and other systems (an example of the latter would be supplier, organization, customer).

GUIDELINES FOR USE

1. When meetings get difficult, ask "Are we dealing with ends or means?" And pursue the answer.

2. Whenever giving project assignments, be careful to separate the ends from the means. Also, when you receive a project assignment, pay close attention to ends and means.

3. If you want to measure success, then measure ends, not means.

(Continued)

GUIDELINES FOR USE *(Concluded)*

4. If you aren't clear on a task, ask why you are doing the task. It will move you toward the ends. Ask again, two or three times, to get to the real ends.

5. In interpersonal matters, if conflict threatens to break out, call a truce and see whether the argument is over whats or hows; then get agreement on the what. Agreement there often mitigates fights over hows.

B. TEACHING AND LEARNING—MEANS AND ENDS

What is the difference between teaching and learning? Teaching is the way to accomplish learning; it is the means. Learning is the outcome; it is the end-goal of teaching. Schools focus on teachers and teaching, but they need to keep in mind the desired outcome—the student's actual learning. Teachers and trainers of all types should ask themselves:

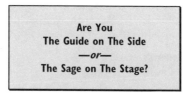

Are You
The Guide on The Side
—or—
The Sage on The Stage?

Facilitators and Platform Presenters are Different!

There are a number of other key distinctions between teaching and learning, as the following table illustrates. (Note that teaching is not solely responsible for all of these outcomes.)

LEARNING AND TEACHING: DISTINCTIONS

Learning (Outcomes)	❖	Teaching (Means)
Andragogy	←————————→	**Pedagogy**
Leader of Man (Adult)		Leader of Child
Self-Directed	Self-Concept	Dependent
Rich	Past Experiences	Little
Social Roles	Readiness	Biological Development
Immediate Application	Time Perspective	Postponed Application
Problem-Centered	Learning Orientation	Subject-Centered
Learner	Locus of Control	Trainer

Always remember to ask the question introduced by this tool: *Are we dealing with the ends (the what) or the means (the how)?* It can serve you well in both your professional and private life.

GUIDELINES FOR USE

1. Recognize this crucial distinction between means and ends, and focus on ends—the learning.

2. Use this tool with later ones to assist with real learning; through active learning processes facilitated by an expert on process.

3. Be careful of "content experts" who have no learning skills beyond "platform presentations." People rarely learn this way.

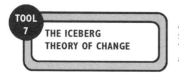

TOOL 7 THE ICEBERG THEORY OF CHANGE

Application of
Standard Systems Dynamics
The Natural Cycles of Life
and Change

When we are changing a system, three elements come into play in all interpersonal and system interactions.

1. The *content* of the change; the change-related tasks and goals

2. The *process* of change; how we carry out the tasks and meet the goals

3. The *structures or framework* within which the content and process operate; the arrangements we must set up to manage change

The first element (content) is obvious: it's what we focus on the most. However, the other two are often difficult to "see," for change is like an iceberg where 87 percent of the issues and solutions are below the surface. The second element (process) lies just below the surface, and the third (structures) lies deep below. As both are essential to success, we must bring them to light by asking:

> **[?]** *What new processes and structures are we using to ensure successful change?*

> ➤ **PRINCIPLE:** The steady-state equilibrium, however much we want it, can be dangerous in a changing world.

Our natural inclination is to maintain the status quo, with its comfort, familiarity, and stability, rather than pursue change, with its awkwardness, uncertainty, and ambiguity.

Change requires us to face the difficult issues of (1) admitting we need to change and being willing to do so, and (2) acquiring new skills and abilities to function more effectvely. But if we have a clear structure for change—a framework and arrangements that help us manage change before it manages us—then both content and process will be easier for us to understand, accept, and work with. Structure operates like a fulcrum:

CONTENT   **PROCESS**

STRUCTURE

Also, knowledge and information are just inputs, and neither is enough of an input to be effective by itself; thus we must develop skills in working with systems if we are to learn and grow as we undergo change. We must consider, too, that short-term creative destruction can at times be the key to long-term advances, and that today's "steady state" is really one of constant change.

➡ **For Example**

Designing, building, and sustaining a customer-focused high-performance learning organization for the 21st century requires a balance in how organizations spend their time and energy between content, processes, and structure.

Above all, what we need to avoid is *content myopia*.

**Content Myopia—
The Failure to Focus on Process and Structures**

Remember: Change is dependent on process and structures!

FIGURE 4. THE WAY TO ACHIEVE THE COMPETITIVE EDGE

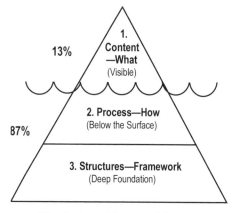

The Iceberg Theory of Change

*Systems change requires a major focus on structure and process
in order to achieve the desired content.*

GUIDELINES FOR USE

1. If you want effective change, then building a change-
    management game plan and a yearly map/project plan
    of the implementation is a must. This is especially true
    if you want to implement a strategic plan. Present the
    latter on the game plan's final page to ensure imple-
    mentation. Also, include key processes and structures in
    the game plan.

2. For help with the process of change, see the Rollercoaster
    of Change in Chapter I; also check out Tool 28.

3. For help with some structures of change, see the menu on
    the next page.

4. Keep track of the changes in your life. Hold a "summit"
    with yourself now and then. Consider holding such
    summits with your family.

PRIIMARY STRATEGIC CHANGE MANAGEMENT
(STRUCTURES AND ROLES)

"A Menu"

1. **Visionary Leadership**—CEO/Senior Executives with Personal Leadership Plans (PLPs)
   - For repetitive stump speeches and reinforcement
   - To ensure integration of all parts & people towards the same vision/values

2. **Internal Support Cadre** (informal/kitchen cabinet)
   - For day-to-day coordination of implementation process
   - To ensure the change structures & processes don't lose out to day-to-day

3. **Executive Committee**
   - For weekly meetings and attention
   - To ensure follow-up on the top 12–25 priority yearly actions from the Strategic Plan

4. **Strategic Change Leadership Steering Committee** (formal)
   - For bimonthly/quarterly follow-up meetings to track, adjust and refine everything (including the Vision)
   - To ensure follow-through via a yearly comprehensive map of implementation

*5. **Strategy Sponsorship Teams**
   - For each core strategy and/or major change effort
   - To ensure achievement of each one; including leadership of what needs to change

*6. **Employee Development Board** (Attunement of People's Hearts)
   - For succession—careers—development—core competencies (all levels)—performance management appraisals
   - To ensure fit with our desired values/culture—and employees as a competitive edge

*7. **Technology Steering Committee/Group**
   - For computer—telecommunications—software fit and integration
   - To ensure "system-wide" coordination around information mangement

(Continued)

PRIIMARY STRATEGIC CHANGE MANAGEMENT
(STRUCTURES AND ROLES) *(concluded)*

*8. **Strategic Communications System (and Structures)**
   - For clear two way dialogue and understanding of the Plan/implementation
   - To ensure everyone is heading in the same direction with the same strategies/values

*9. **Measurement and Benchmarking Team**
   - For collecting and reporting of Key Success Factors, especially customers, employees, competitors
   - To ensure an outcome/customer-focus at all times

10. **Annual Department Plans**
   - For clear and focused department plans that are critiqued, shared, and reviewed
   - To ensure a fit, coordination, and commitment to the core strategies and annual top priorities

11. **Whole System Participation**
   - For input and involvement of all key stakeholders before a decision affecting them is made. Includes Parallel Processes, Search Conferences, management conferences, etc.
   - To ensure a critical mass in support of the vision and desired changes

*Subcommittees of $4: the Leadership Steering Committee

TOOL 8

BUY-IN AND STAY-IN

Application of
Standard Systems Dynamics
— 6. Entropy

We must regularly focus on using feedback to reverse systems entropy—the normal tendency of a system to run down and deteriorate over time. Lack of buy-in isn't the killer here: it's lack of stay-in over time. Therefore we need to ask:

 What must we do to ensure buy-in and stay-in over time (perseverance), and thus avoid entropy?

All business problems conform to the laws of inertia—the longer you wait to look at a problem, the harder it is to correct.

- *Entropy* is the tendency for any system to run down and eventually become inert.

- *Incremental degradation* is the "inroad" of entropy—and the main barrier to achieving the "fit" of all organization processes and actions with the organization's espoused values and vision.

Thus for any system to be effective and maintain stay-in, it must receive attention, booster shots, stop checks, and so forth on a regular basis.

> **PRINCIPLE: If entropy is not reversed, the system will die.**

Systems can continuously increase in complexity until they become bureaucratic and ossified, ultimately resulting in the death of the system. All living systems require the constant inputs of energy and feedback if they are to reverse such entropy. Sometimes the chaos and disorder of a system presents a discouraging picture, but as Meg Wheatley discusses in her recent book, these are often precursors to renewal and growth at a higher level.

 For Example

> While human beings obviously have a finite life cycle, it doesn't have to be this way for neighborhoods, communities, and organizations. For them, the renewal process that reverses the entropy is key to long-term success.

The role of feedback here is the good news, for in our world of instantly accessible information networks, we have an almost limitless supply of constant feedback to provide us with new inputs toward change. However, there is a downside to this situation, as we often hit information overload, which leads to more complexity in our lives.

The Telltale Signs of Organizational Entropy

How do you know if your organization is experiencing entropy? The following list, from DePree and Miller (1987), presents the telltale signs.

- A tendency toward formality and politeness versus effectiveness
- Turf battles among key people
- No longer having time for celebrations and recognition
- A growing feeling that achieving goals is the same as a reward
- When people stop telling legendary stories of the founders and other key people
- The acceptance of complexity and ambiguity, and the ability as normal and acceptable
- Promotion of people just like you

- When people begin to have different meanings of words like *quality,* or *service,* or *customer*
- When problem-solvers become mainly reactive
- Managers who seek to control rather than empower others
- When the pressure of day-to-day operations pushes aside our concern for vision and long-time direction
- An orientation toward the traditional rules of MBAs and engineering logic alone rather than taking into account such things as contribution, spirit, excellence, beauty, and joy
- When people think of customers as problems rather than as opportunities to serve
- Thick policy manuals and job description
- Leaders who rely on structures instead of people
- A loss of confidence in judgment of the leaders by the rank and file and wisdom
- increased rudeness
- A focus on forecasting versus planning

Building a Critical Mass for Change

Normally change leaders focus on buy-in to create a critical mass for change. It can up to two years to build the critical mass for large-scale change. Here are some ways to do it.

1. Modify drafts of the strategic plan. Review the plan, and share and gain feedback from the people affected by it.

2. Throughout planning and implementation, hold feedback meetings with your key stakeholders in parallel with your thinking and decision making; not later in the sequence.

3. Develop trust in your leadership by being open to feedback through a Strategic Change Leadership steering committee. If there are any skeptics, get them talking, and listen to them.

4. Develop three-year business plans for all business units and major support departments, involving key stakeholders and staff as well.

5. Develop annual plans for all departments, divisions, and sections under the strategic plan/core strategy umbrella.

6. Put out updates after each meeting of the strategic change steering committee, and ask for feedback.

7. Use strategic sponsorship teams as change agents for each core strategy/major change.

8. Implement quick changes and actions so people know you are serious once you start the change.

9. Review reward systems and the performance appraisal form to reinforce core values and core strategies.

10. Answer the question "What in it for me?" (WIIFM) for each person affected by the change. In this way you take into consideration many issues, from political to cultural, that may affect the success of the change.

"Skeptics Are My Best Friends"

Remember that skeptics can be your best friends here. If you encounter skeptics at any level, be sure to ask them why they believe the changes will not work out. Get them to identify what they see as the roadblocks to the change, and listen to what they have to say—don't argue or try to force them to agree with you. It may turn out that those road-blocks are the key items you will need to overcome to ensure the successful achievement of your vision and then most skeptics will buy and and stay in.

The following shows a two-year profile for building the support needed to create the critical mass.

Year 1. *Involves* . . .
- Core Strategic Planning/Major Change Team
- Plus 20 to 40 key "others"
- The collective management team

Year 2. *Involves* . . .
- The rest of the organization
- Other key external stakeholders

Institutionalizing the Desired Changes

Getting long-term stay-in on change projects requires institutionalizing the desired changes. Ways to do this include the following:

1. Conduct an organizational assessment to see the status of the change and whether there are any problems that need addressing for the change to reach its full effectiveness.

2. Conduct refresher-training courses on the change topic.

3. Hold yearly conferences on the subject (renewal).

4. Make the basic change and any further needed improvements (see item 1) a part of senior line management's goals and performance appraisal.

5. Conduct a reward system's diagnosis and make appropriate changes so that the rewards (both financial and non-financial) are congruent and consistent with the changes.

6. Set up an ongoing audit system. Also find ways to statistically measure the change effectiveness. Line managers are used to statistics and generally like them.

7. Ensure you have ways to discuss and reinforce the change at periodic staff meetings of top management and department heads.

8. Put the changes into organizational policies and procedures; then make someone accountable for them. Set up permanent jobs to update the changes, or put the accountability into existing job descriptions.

9. Use a variety of communications avenues and processes for both one-way and two-way feedback on the change.

10. Hold periodic team meetings on the subject across the organization.

11. Have top line managers regularly conduct "deep-sensing" meetings on the subject, down into the organization.

12. Hold periodic intergroup or interdepartment meetings on the subject and its status.

13. Set up a process for annually renewing and reexamining the change in order to improve it on a continuing basis.

14. Have outside consultants conduct periodic visits on the subject and assess the status of the change.

15. Be doubly sure that the top team continues to model the changes. (You can "refreeze" this through many other items on this list.)

16. Set priorities and deadlines for short-term change improvements.

17. Look closely at the key environmental sectors to be sure they are reinforcing the changes. (Pay particular attention to any parent companies or division heads.)

18. Create physical indications of the permanency of the change; for example, offices, jobs, brochures.

19. Develop "stay agents" or multiple persons who have a strong interest in maintaining the change. (Do this particularly among line managers and informal leaders.)

20. Refine change procedures to make them routine and normal.

21. Link other organizational systems to the change.

Encourage specific and formal communications, coordination, and processes between them.

22. Keep the goals and benefits of the change clear and well known.

23. Assess the potential dangers and pitfalls of the change, and develop specific approaches and plans to minimize these dangers.

24. Be alert to other changes that can negatively affect this change—such as unintended side effects and other consequences.

25. Don't have the person who manages the stability also manage the change. These are two different tasks, calling for different personalities. Each one should be given its own separate manager. It only makes sense that change agents are poor stay agents!

GUIDELINES FOR USE

I. Turn to this tool whenever you need help with the practical necessities of getting buy-in and long-term stay-in. Use it to help others understand the often-overlooked value of stay-in.

2. Ensure that others in your organization understand the concept of entropy and its effects on an organization. Take a good look at your organization. Do you see entropy at work? Also ,make sure that others understand that entropy can be reversed and lead to renewal and growth at a higher level.

3. Remember to make "skeptics your best friends" as detailed here.

4. Expect entropy to occur in every new change you introduce. Thus, build in specific points to provide booster shots/check points.

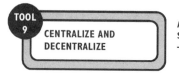

Application of
Standard Systems Dynamics
— 10. Interrelated Parts

Build strategic consistency and operational flexibility into your organization. Focus on what is strategic (the "what" or ends) and what is operational (the "how" or means); avoid thinking in terms of centralize *versus* decentralize—it's too simplistic. One size no longer fits all; consistency is not always key, especially in the "how." Being strategically consistent in your vision or mission, and operationally flexible through empowerment, are the successors to the traditional centralized versus decentralized dilemma.

This leads us to the systems question:

> **[?]** *What should we centralize and what should we decentralize?*

Usually centralization will focus mostly on whats and decentralization on the hows.

> ▶ PRINCIPLE: There are many different ways to achieve the same desired outcomes. Principle: People support what they help create.

We need to put this systems principle into action by encouraging those who will be affected by the change to contribute input to the planning process prior to implementing the change. We also need decision makers who are willing to accept such input and work with it—leaders who understand that people naturally want to be involved in decisions that will have an impact on them, and who see the advantage in receiving people's input. The input increases buy-in and stay-in (tool #8) and *also* often provides better answers from these closest to the issues. Such leaders know that thinking in terms of "one best way" simply doesn't work, and that participatory management skills are required.

➡ **Example**

Today's leadership paradigm calls for a new way of looking at organizations. It requires a much higher level of maturity and wisdom—a middle ground between abdicating responsibility and being all controlling—with a focus on interdependence.

The Three Levels of Maturity and Wisdom

3. Interdependent (Systems/Teamwork)
2. Independent (Individual/Separate)
I. Dependent (Childlike)

GUIDELINES FOR USE

I. Leaders need to define the few things they must have to ensure consistency in their organizations; for example, organizational values and beliefs, shared vision and/or mission, and key strategies everyone should help carry out.

2. Most organizations need consistency in the following few areas: financial arrangements, senior executives/succession planning, organization identity and visibility, and positioning in the marketplace vs. the competition with your customers. Beyond these few strategic consistencies, operational flexibility and empowerment should reign.

3. In our personal lives, we need tolerance for others, such as family members, allowing them the flexibility to live their lives as they want as long as they stay true to agreed-upon values.

TOOL 10 — MULTIPLE CAUSES: ROOT CAUSES

Application of
Standard Systems Dynamics
— 2. Open Systems
— 11. Dynamic Equilibrium
— 12. Internal Elaboration

It is important to use free-flowing and participative-management and active-learning techniques to find the linkages and multiple causality factors that are the root causes of problems and other concerns. The question we begin with is simple:

[?] *What multiple causes lie at the root of our problem or concern? (That is, what are the root causes?)*

Answering it is seldom easy, though, for it's difficult to detect root causes, and we are often unaware of their long-term impact on our lives. If you, as a manager, were to illustrate some factors that have a long-term impact on what you do each day, the result might look like this:

Long-Term Impact on What You Do Each Day

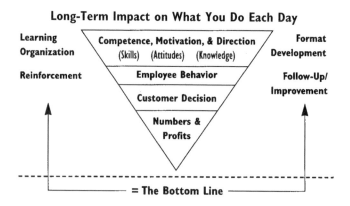

> ➤ **PRINCIPLE:** Root causes and their effects are usually not linked closely in time and space.

A cause rarely makes a direct, immediate impact on every effect it is linked to. Furthermore, there is rarely a single cause behind anything in this world, whether it be a problem, a human being, or a rainstorm. Most of us know this in the abstract (or at least sense it); yet in practice, we still *think* in terms of immediate, singular causes and effects—which is an outmoded, mechanization-oriented way of thinking.

➡ **Example**

On the organizational problem-solving front, such thinking leads to the search for fast, convenient solutions—quick fixes—as if we were dealing with simple mechanical objects, not unwanted outcomes in a system within systems.

Our simplistic cause-effect analyses, especially when coupled with the desire for quick fixes, usually lead to far more problems than they solve—impatience and knee-jerk reactions included. If we stop for a moment and take a good look our world and its seven levels of complex and interdependent systems, we begin to understand that *multiple causes with multiple effects* are the true reality, as are *circles of causality-effects.*

➡ **Example**

Consider how our weather and crops are affected by multiple causes such as these:
- The oceans—moderators of climate
- Atmospheric forces—for instance, the jet streams
- Various combinations of the above—such as El Niño
- Rain forests—high generators of weather
- Geological activity—such as volcanic eruptions (even very distant ones)

Delay time, the time between causes and their impacts, can highly influence systems. Yet the concept of delayed effect is often missed in our impatient society, and when it *is* recognized, it's almost always underestimated. Such oversight and devaluation can lead to poor decision making as well as poor problem solving, for decisions often have consequences that don't show up until years later. Fortunately, mind mapping, fishbone diagrams, and creativity/brainstorming tools can be quite useful here.

Keep in mind, though, that *the complexity encountered in this area is often far beyond our human ability to fully assess and comprehend.* Thus it is crucial to flag or anticipate delays, understand and appreciate them, and learn to work *with* them rather than against them.

➡ **Example**

Most of us actually work with such delays all the time, and base decisions on them. Investments, pensions, savings, and the like all have delayed effects—ones we bet our futures on. However, we seldom see that delayed effect plays a crucial role in other decision-making and problem-solving areas of our lives.

GUIDELINES FOR USE

1. The training and development function has many active learning techniques that will help you find root causes. Involve people affected by a change in the search for these causes and for solutions.

2. Use these techniques to search for root causes, not superficial symptoms. Some root causes are very hard to find. Continually ask, "What else might be a root cause?" and ask "why" over and over again.

3. Keep an open-systems view of the environment, as it often contributes to the root causes as well.

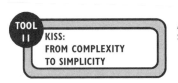

Application of
Standard Systems Dynamics
— 7. Equifinality
— 9. Hierarchy
—12. Internal Elaboration

A. REDUCING BUREAUCRACY

Flexibility, adaptability, speed, and simplicity are far preferable to rigid plans, tight controls, one-size-fits-all consistency, and economies of scale. We need to eliminate the waste of complexity and bureaucracy and try to flatten system hierarchies. This requires us to ask:

> *How can we move from complexity to simplicity, and from consistency to flexibility, in the solutions we devise?*

➡ **Example**

To get an idea of how bureaucracy (and analytic thinking) has run amuck in our lives, see Chapter I, section "Systems Thinking Versus 'Machine Age' Thinking."

★ THE GOAL (IN WHATEVER WE DO) ★
Clarify & Simplify—Clarify & Simplify—Clarify & Simplify

> ➤ **PRINCIPLE:** Multilevel systems are too complex to fully understand and manage centrally.

Privatization and free-market economies generally work because those closest to the action of a business are allowed to make decisions for the business. We need to carry this principle over into big business (and big government as well), realizing that it is the thousands of little decisions we all make daily in our businesses that shape and meet market needs, not "higher-up" dictates or regulations. Clearly, "corporate central" has a role to play in the success of businesses, but it should not be an all-encompassing one. Corporate bureacracies should be shaped into smaller units, so that the people who work *in* the units—the ones that best understand the units' operations and needs—have enough freedom to act on that understanding. In fact, we may find in the future that virtual corporations work more effectively than traditional, vertically integrated and complex ones.

The KISS ("Keep it simple, stupid") method is more powerful than many economies of scale. This method begins with us and the questions we bring to our organizations.

GUIDELINES FOR USE

I. **To reduce bureaucracy and create simplicity and flexibility, answer these 10 questions in terms of your own job or life.**

1. *What made me angry today?*
2. *What took too long?*
3. *What caused complaints?*
4. *What was misunderstood?*
5. *What cost too much?*
6. *What was wanted?*
7. *What was too complicated?*
8. *What was just plain silly?*
9. *What job took too many people?*
10. *What job took too many actions?*

2. **Ask yourself these three questions to build in simplicity.**

1. *What is going well in my organization or personal life, and so should not be changed?*
2. *What are the abrasive or problem areas that should be examined?*
3. *If I could change my organization/my life with a "stroke of the pen," what would I change?*

B. THE RULE OF THREES

In viewing the world, we usually organize things into threes—for instance: sun, moon, stars; land, air, water. This a natural human tendency, perhaps because thirds offer us the simplest conceptual balance in seeing a whole. When dealing with human constructs, we thus find threes used everywhere as a principle of order and comprehension (many of us even see ourselves as comprising three parts—body, mind, and spirit). The KISS method adopts this tendency, the Rule of Threes, as a primary way to "keep it simple."

MANAGEMENT'S ULTIMATE CHALLENGE
Search for the simplicity on the far side of complexity

➡ **Example**

Here are some applications of the Rule of Threes:

- Individual: Body, mind, spirit
- Learning: Skills, knowledge, feeling/attitude
- Human Interaction: Structure, content, process

GUIDELINES FOR USE

1. Whenever you are trying to influence someone, order your views into three main points. Most people will find them easier to remember. (This is a good technique for talks or presentations, too.)

2. In all you do, ask yourself, "What are my three main points?" Build frameworks people can remember.

3. When someone is being complex or rambling on, ask the person for his or her three main points or, if appropriate, for three "pro" points and three "con" points.

4. As Steve Covey asks in his 7 Habits book (1989), "What is the third Alternative?" This often helps to stop artificial and competitive win-lose options and conflicts.

TOOL
12
The Ultimate Question:
SUPERORDINATE
GOALS

Application of
Standard Systems Dynamics
— 6. Multiple Outcomes
— 9. Hierarchy

To paraphrase Albert Einstein, problems can't be solved at the level they were created; so we need to go to the next-higher systems level and its desired outcome in order to succeed. By using higher-systems-order outcomes, we focus on abundance (win-win activities), rather than scarcity (win-lose). To initiate that focus, we ask:

> **?** ***What is our common higher-level***
> ***(superordinate) goal?***

To raise new questions, new possibilities, to regard old problems from a new angle, requires creative imagination and marks real advance in science.

—Albert Einstein

> **PRINCIPLE:** **Problems cannot be solved at the level they were created.**

This is the ultimate systems principle. It requires that we advance beyond analytical thinking to *genuine* systems thinking in order to resolve our issues. Climb into a mental helicopter and rise to a higher level to gain a broader perspective and a high purpose and a wider range of solutions.

➡ Example

Union-management fights and strikes over pay tend to amount to a win-lose game. By moving to the higher-level goal of competing and producing more profitably, both sides can make more money (increase the size of the pie).

It is also important to apply the ultimate systems principle to our personal lives.

➡ **Example**

In your day-to-day life, do you think about your future vision and your higher-level goals?

If you do not think about the future, you cannot have one.
—John Galsworthy

GUIDELINES FOR USE

I. Whenever it feels like a discussion is going nowhere, ask "What is the common superordinate goal that everyone can support?"

2. Ask the above question when you are planning daily, weekly, monthly, or yearly schedules. Get everyone involved in the planning to work on the answer. Sometimes this is seen as a "shared vision or core strategies."

APPLICATIONS

III. Phase A:
The Outcome-Thinking Tools

The two applications in this chapter center on Phase A of
the A-B-C-D Systems Model: output and the future state.
As we have seen, the question associated with this phase is:

> **Where do we want to be?**
> (What are our outcomes? purposes? goals?)

These Phase A tools offer you key, practical assistance in
becoming outcome/results-oriented and customer-focused.

TOOL NO.	THE APPLICATIONS
13.	Focus on Outcomes
14.	Customer Focus
➡ These Tools Will Help You Become Outcome-Oriented!	

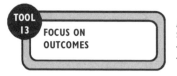

TOOL
13
FOCUS ON
OUTCOMES

Application of
Standard Systems Dynamics
— 4. Input-Output
— 6. Multiple Outcomes

Focusing on outcomes means defining and meeting
customer wants and needs. The value to the customer
is always a mix of five outcomes:

- Choice and customization
- Service excellence, ease of doing business
- High-quality goods and services
- Speed, timeliness, responsiveness
- Total cost (in all ways)

The "star model," below, shows these outcomes in an easy-
to-remember form. Outstanding strength in any of these
outcomes can help you gain an advantageous position in the
marketplace.

FIGURE 5. CUSTOMER-VALUE STAR MODEL

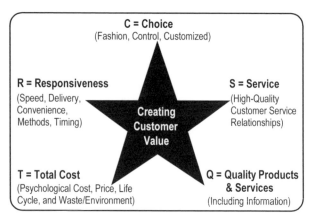

The Customer-Value Assessment Instrument

Use the following instrument to assess what your customers currently value (later, in this tool's guidelines, we will look at optional uses for the instrument). Once you have your assessment results, write a competitive-positioning statement of what differentiates you from your competition—a statement that indicates your core competitive strategy.

CUSTOMER-VALUE ASSESSMENT						
Assess. of What Customer Values / Custom. Segments	Score 1 (Low) to 10 (High)					Overall Comments
	1. Choice (Control)	2. Service (Relationships)	3. Quality Products & Services	4. Responsiveness	5. Total Cost	
1.						
2.						
3.						
4.						
5.						
6.						
7.						

Competitive-Positioning

An organization's competitive positioning may also be called its driving force, strategic intent, or grand strategy; it is sometimes referred to as "the mother of all core strategies." Such strategy is the main way we achieve a sustained competitive edge over the competition. In developing your competitive-positioning statement, you should capture that way in clear and precise terms, keeping in mind the information below.

- To avoid competitive disadvantage, you must focus the strategic thrust on one or two customer values; any more than that and you're attempting to be "all things to all people." The other customer-desired values of the Star Model should be accomplished at just the level needed to be competitive.

- This positioning is the key strategic thrust in your vision and mission statements. All other functions, directions, decisions, and criteria are subordinate to it. Competitive positioning also is (or can be):

  — The organization's core or distinctive competency
  — The *who, what,* or *how* of your mission and values (*why* is a given)
  — The organization's current reality or possible reality within a planned period of time
  — What the organization is known for—its reputation or distinctiveness
  — What the organization's rallying cry is derived from, and what it reinforces
  — Something sustainable as an edge over a period of years and not readily duplicated

A Closing Note on Positioning

Remember that competitive business advantages are difficult to achieve. Sustainable advantage requires the organization to build and deliver a capability that others cannot duplicate easily or quickly. Therefore you can gain a competitive advantage only by doing something difficult; if it's easy to do, too many other people can do it also.

GUIDELINES FOR USE

I. You also can use the customer-value assessment instrument to assess the following:

    • What you anticipate your customers will value in the near or far future

    • How you are currently meeting customer value

    • Where you desire your competitive positioning to be on the assessment matrix

2. Don't forget to write a position statement after using the assessment instrument.

3. Another option is to use the assessment instrument on a personal level to assess your own career. Whom do you serve? And how well do you provide these value outcomes to your organization? If you investigate this option, be sure to write a competitive-positioning statement once you receive your results. This positioning should be what differentiates you from your competition.

TOOL 14

CUSTOMER FOCUS

Application of
Standard Systems Dynamics
— 4. Input-Output

The only reason for the existence of any organization is to serve someone else. This is your primary outcome. Thus once you've identified your customer, the organization's entire focus should be on serving that customer.

➡ For Example

If Cadillac has upscale older folks as its customers, the total organization—its people, plant, products—should be focused on those customers.

➡ For Example

If part of your purpose in life is to raise your children well, then you must focus on them properly, giving them quality time, ensuring they receive a good education, instilling values in them, and so on.

The "Ten Commandments" of a Customer-Focused Organization

One way to focus on outcomes is to see whether your organization is a customer-focused one. Best-practices research has shown there are 10 primary indicators of a customer-focused organization. They are presented as commandments in the following rating sheet (see next page).

Rate your organization on each commandment, using a scale from 1 (low) to 10 (high); then simply tally your total score. Pay attention to the commandments your organization did not score well on, and work to improve those areas of weakness. Celebrate that which you do well.

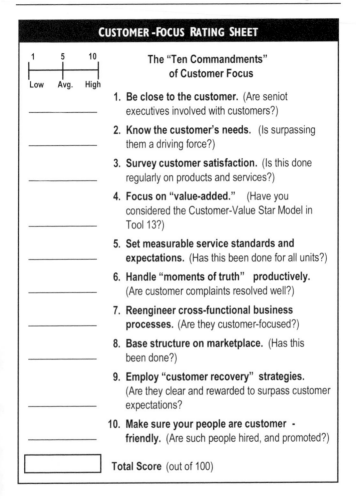

CUSTOMER-FOCUS RATING SHEET

```
1     5     10
|-----|------|
Low   Avg.  High
```

The "Ten Commandments" of Customer Focus

1. **Be close to the customer.** (Are seniot executives involved with customers?)

2. **Know the customer's needs.** (Is surpassing them a driving force?)

3. **Survey customer satisfaction.** (Is this done regularly on products and services?)

4. **Focus on "value-added."** (Have you considered the Customer-Value Star Model in Tool 13?)

5. **Set measurable service standards and expectations.** (Has this been done for all units?)

6. **Handle "moments of truth" productively.** (Are customer complaints resolved well?)

7. **Reengineer cross-functional business processes.** (Are they customer-focused?)

8. **Base structure on marketplace.** (Has this been done?)

9. **Employ "customer recovery" strategies.** (Are they clear and rewarded to surpass customer expectations?)

10. **Make sure your people are customer-friendly.** (Are such people hired, and promoted?)

Total Score (out of 100)

"Moments of Truth" and Customer Recovery Strategy

Handling "moments of truth" (the sixth commandment) and employing customer recovery strategy (CRS; the ninth commandment) are the keys to providing unsurpassed customer service. If customers are happy with you, they tell three or four people; if unhappy, they tell a dozen or more. Thus a major issue for any organization is how to handle customer problems and complaints in a productive, customer-satisfying way.

➡ **For Example**

Each problem or complaint has a story behind it, which the customer will tell to friends. The question is, how will the story end? On a good note, or a bad one? The bottom line is, if the story ends well, both the organization and the customer benefit.

Checklist: Moments of Truth

The checklist below comprises a number of essentials for providing unsurpassed customer service. How many do you act on when a customer-related problem occurs?

CHECKLIST: MOMENTS OF TRUTH
❑ Focus on the 5-to-10-year ROI of the customer.
❑ Focus on your long-term image and reputation.
❑ Empower employees to be creative and innovative at the "moment of truth," so you will surpass the customer's expectations for solutions to the problem.
❑ Provide expenditure authority to do the above.
❑ Ensure accountability equals responsibility.

(Continued)

> ### CHECKLIST: MOMENTS OF TRUTH *(Concluded)*
>
> ❑ Focus recovery on future business (e.g., 50 percent price reduction or free next time).
>
> ❑ Speed up the recovery—at the "moment of truth."
>
> ❑ Develop a "customer guarantee" and live up to it or surpass it.
>
> ❑ Ensure your CRS has measures in place for quick response, knowledgeability, and empathy and sensitivity, as well as tangibles and other intangibles.

Mastery of Customer Recovery Strategy

There are four levels of responses to customer problems and complaints, ranging from undesirable responses to CRS mastery.

The Four Levels of Response to Customer Problems

1. Deny it's our problem. ("We just work here.")

2. Fight the customers' concerns but eventually give in to them. ("They won.")

3. Meet customer expectations. ("The customer is always right.")

4. Meet customer expectations; then do something extra that the customer doesn't expect (including offering an apology).

At what level are you now operating? What might you do to attain a higher level? What improvement steps are needed? Answer these questions using the following CRS checklist and worksheet.

CRS CHECKLIST AND WORKSHEET

PRESENT LEVEL

CRS LEVELS

Low ❑ 1. Deny it's our problem. ("We just work here.")

❑ 2. Fight the customers' concerns but eventually give in to them. ("They won.")

❑ 3. Meet customer expectations. ("The customer is always right.")

High ❑ 4. Meet customer expectations; then do something extra that the customer doesn't expect (including offering an apology).

LEVEL DESIRED:

IMPROVEMENT STEPS NEEDED:

GUIDELINES FOR USE

1. Have others in your organization fill out the Customer-Focus Rating Sheet, and compare results. Look into any discrepancies between them, build on agreed-upon strengths, and work to improve areas of weakness.

2. Also share the CRS Checklist and Worksheet with others in the organization, and work together on the steps to any needed improvements.

 **APPLICATIONS**

IV. Phase B:
Feedback and Learning Tools

The two applications in this chapter center on Phase B of the A-B-C-D Systems Model: feedback loop. As we have seen, the question associated with this phase is:

 How will we know we have reached our outcomes, purposes, or goals?

With these Phase B tools, you will better understand the connections between feedback and learning, and get a good idea of what is involved in creating a learning organization.

TOOL NO.	THE APPLICATIONS
15.	Feedback and Learning
16.	Reinforcement and the Learning Organizaton
➡ These Tools Will Help You Bring Learning to the Organization!	

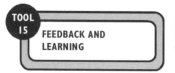

TOOL
15   FEEDBACK AND
     LEARNING

Application of
Standard Systems Dynamics
— 5. Feedback

A. FEEDBACK

Feedback loops should be created for all systems levels
(e.g., individuals, teams, HR programs, business processes)
and used regularly to measure desired outcomes and actual
success versus planned success. Each person in the company
should take some time each week to reflect on what he or
she has learned through these loops.

> **Feedback = Learning = Learning Organization**
> *Feedback is "the breakfast of champions" Learning consists*
> *of knowledge, skills, and attitude*

It is important to understand that knowledge itself is an
input, and that learning comprises not just *knowledge,* but
also *skills* and *attitude.* You cannot use the knowledge of
how to meet a clearly defined and agreed-upon objective
unless you also possess the skills (abilities and readiness) to
carry through on that knowledge and have the attitude
(willingness or desire) needed to do so.

In Systems Terms

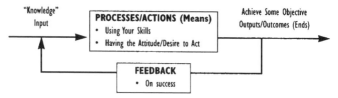

"Knowledge"
Input

PROCESSES/ACTIONS (Means)
• Using Your Skills
• Having the Attitude/Desire to Act

Achieve Some Objective
Outputs/Outcomes (Ends)

FEEDBACK
• On success

GUIDELINES FOR USE

Ask yourself and your team if there is a feedback mechanism in place for everything you and they do, and if each mechanism offers a way to turn information into new learnings and new applications. Also ask whether people in your organization improve skills and attitude. (Keep in mind that this requires *practice*—not one-hour or one-day briefings.)

B. LEARNING

Figure 6 shows how knowledge, skills, and attitude come together in the learning of managerial effectiveness. A

FIGURE 6. Managerial Effectiveness Triangle

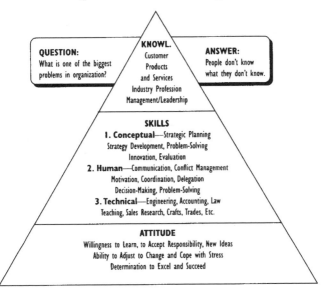

QUESTION:
What is one of the biggest problems in organization?

KNOWL.
Customer
Products
and Services
Industry Profession
Management/Leadership

ANSWER:
People don't know what they don't know.

SKILLS
I. **Conceptual**—Strategic Planning
Strategy Development, Problem-Solving
Innovation, Evaluation
2. **Human**—Communication, Conflict Management
Motivation, Coordination, Delegation
Decision-Making, Problem-Solving
3. **Technical**—Engineering, Accounting, Law
Teaching, Sales Research, Crafts, Trades, Etc.

ATTITUDE
Willingness to Learn, to Accept Responsibility, New Ideas
Ability to Adjust to Change and Cope with Stress
Determination to Excel and Succeed

more detailed view of learning in general is shown in
Figure 7, "The Stairway to Learning." Use it to examine
your own growth and development as a life-long learner
in all types of human dimensions.

GUIDELINES FOR USE

1. Recognize the different kinds of learnings and the steps
    involved in learning and applying new knowledge and
    skills. (For a four-page article on this topic, contact the
    Centre for Strategic Management at 619-275-6528).

2. Teach the Stairway of Learning to your family, team, and
    organization. Be especially aware of Step 1: "You don't
    know what you don't know." Finding organizational "best
    practices" is the most effective way to get beyond Step 1.

C. UNDERSTANDING THE THREE COMPONENTS OF LEARNING

Most of us don't really understanding learning and their
combined role of knowledge, skills, and attitude. We know
much more about the activity of teaching, which is only one
method for helping people learn. A brief primer on basics:

> ### "Adults Learn Best by Doing"
>
> But to really learn from experience, you must
> process the experience. Otherwise, you may
> "learn" the wrong thing.

FIGURE 7. THE STAIRWAY OF LEARNING

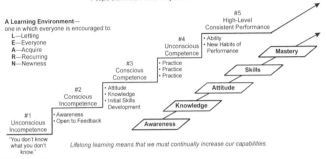

"People Don't Know What They Don't Know"

A Learning Environment—
one in which everyone is encouraged to:
L—Letting
E—Everyone
A—Acquire
R—Recurring
N—Newness

#5
High-Level
Consistent Performance

#4
Unconscious
Competence
• Ability
• New Habits of
  Performance

Mastery

#3
Conscious
Competence
• Practice
• Practice
• Practice

Skills

#2
Conscious
Incompetence
• Attitude
• Knowledge
• Initial Skills
  Development

Attitude

Knowledge

#1
Unconscious
Incompetence
• Awareness
• Open to Feedback

Awareness

"You don't know
what you don't
know."

Lifelong learning means that we must continually increase our capabilities.

SOURCE: Jim Mckinlay, Partner, Centre for Strategic Management

Exercise: What Do You Do Well to Facilitate Learning?

Ask yourself, "What do I, or we as an organization, do well
in the area of learning?" Answer by distributing 10 points
across the learning components, shown below.

Learning Components	How It Is Today	How You Want It to Be
1. Knowledge	_____	_____
2. Skills	_____	_____
3. Attitude	_____	_____
Total Points	10	10

GUIDELINES FOR USE

1. **What are you teaching and changing? How are you doing it? Consider these questions in light of the following:**

    Focus of Change   **How to Influence Change**

    Information/Knowledge ....Lecture/Video

    Skills .... Demonstration/Practice

    Attitude .... Group Discussion

    Behavior.. Feedback Experience

2. **Consider experiential lectures and participative training techniques as a way to facilitate learning. Here are some possibilities:**

Lecturettes	Demonstrations	Brainstorming
Models with	Role playing	Action planning
ice-breakers	Simulations	Case studies
Dyads/triads	Structured	Instruments
Buzz groups	experiences	Problem analysis
Subgroups	Questionnaires	Films/AV with
Task forces	and surveys	follow-up discussion
Games/skits	Fish bowl	Active listening

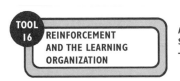

TOOL 16 · REINFORCEMENT AND THE LEARNING ORGANIZATION

Application of
Standard Systems Dynamics
— 5. Feedback

A. REINFORCEMENT OF LEARNING

Are you trying to create a learning organization? Or are you just trying to maximize your retention of the learning experiences you have? In either case, you need to pay attention to the need for continuous feedback and reinforcement of learning.

There are a variety of methods for sustaining new behaviors, including challenge, recognition, and support. Repetition is also a key factor in reinforcement! You should build these methods into all of your learning events and learning opportunities.

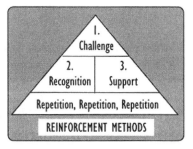

Yearly Reinforcement, Bit by Bit

Reinforcing training in bite-sized chunks is an excellent way to approach this necessity. Use a 52-week reinforcement program, organizing it as shown in a sample on the next page. Record the topic of learning and the other details you need to ensure the learning efforts in your organization meet with long-term success.

FIGURE 8. SAMPLE: 52-WEEK TRAINING REINFORCEMENT PROGRAM

TOPIC	WEEK	TRAINER	TIME
1.			
2.			
3.			
4.			

GUIDELINES FOR USE

Other follow-up ideas for learning reinforcement include:

- **Contracting for challenge/support**

- **Setting up a buddy system, lunches, and so on. Use a free-floating agenda, built at each meeting.**

- **Creating small groups or teams to teach and review each learning, to see what is working and what is not**

- **Following up every few months (holding "alumni sessions")**

B. MINI-TEAM FEEDBACK—RULE OF THREE

At the end of every group meeting and training session, you should hold a mini-feedback session, at least two or three minutes long, on how the meeting process (not content) went and how to learn from it and improve it. This mini-session acts as a meeting-processing guide. Use the following threefold formula as an introduction:

In looking at the time frame of this meeting, and to make the next meeting's process work even more (or as) effectively, I recommend we . . .

1. Continue to do the following: [supply details].
2. Do more of [or begin doing] the following: [supply details].
3. Do less of [or stop doing] the following: [supply details].

GUIDELINES FOR USE

1. At the end of every meeting, conference, or team/project effort, use the mini-session threefold formula. It only takes a few minutes to do this, and it gets you useful feedback to improve whatever you are doing.

2. Close the mini-session by asking, "If you were to talk to a good friend about this meeting, what would you tell him or her about it?"

C. THE LEARNING ORGANIZATION

There are a number of elements integral to organizing and creating a learning organization, many of which are included in the learning-organization checklist on the following page. When you are attempting this kind of change, it is important to realize that the organization's internal capacity for responding to and initiating change is linked to its capacity for learning, feedback and organizational renewal.

➡ **For Example**

Systems design and redesign call for the capacity for renewal, because as soon as a design is *implemented,* its *consequences* indicate a need for redesign. Therefore:

1. *A learning system must be built in to whatever restructuring you do.*
2. *Adapting processes (debriefing, ongoing feedback) must be developed and implemented.*

As this example suggests, the best system is an *inexact* adaptive-learning, ideal-seeking system. Such a system helps you deal constructively with the problem of entropy (see Chapter I for more on this topic) and ensures the organization's capacity for renewal meets its crucial need.

CHECKLIST: CREATING THE LEARNING ORGANIZATION

Directions: Many of the elements needed to create and organize a learning organization are listed below. Which ones does your organization need? Check off the elements, rating your need from high (H) to medium (M) to low (L).

H - M - L	ACTIONS NEEDED
☐ ☐ ☐	1. Reward managers who try to create it.
☐ ☐ ☐	2. Process meetings at the end to improve them.
☐ ☐ ☐	3. Conduct training and learning experiences at each staff meeting.
☐ ☐ ☐	4. Create "whole jobs" with direct customer contact. Give people the autonomy and freedom to act on and control their own jobs ("Every employee a manager").
☐ ☐ ☐	5. Provide everyone with jobs/tasks that include OJT and new learning experiences.
☐ ☐ ☐	6. Conduct lots of training with follow-up and applications review, so it is meaningful and useful to people's jobs.
☐ ☐ ☐	7. Understand and use adult learning theory as a way to present any and all new situations. Supply people with questions, not solutions.
☐ ☐ ☐	8. Set up a 52-week training program (bite-sized learning).
☐ ☐ ☐	9. Set up periodic and regular personal feedback for employees on how they come across to others and on their job performance as related to objectives.
☐ ☐ ☐	10. Set up a strategic management-development system for all management levels. Use managers/executives as the trainers to help others learn better.
☐ ☐ ☐	11. Train and evaluate managers and executives in their new role of TLC—trainer, leader, coach.

(Continued)

CHECKLIST: CREATING THE LEARNING ORGANIZATION *(Concluded)*		
H - M - L		**ACTIONS NEEDED**
☐ ☐ ☐	12.	Work daily on continuous performance improvement and delegation, and track it.
☐ ☐ ☐	13.	Set up debriefings and postmartums to ensure people learn from their mistakes and experiences.
☐ ☐ ☐	14.	Help the organization develop a culture of forgiveness and problem-solving, rather than one of blame. Promote experimentation, discovery, and mistake making as a way to learn.
☐ ☐ ☐	15.	Inspire a shared vision/common purpose that people can relate to and enthusiastically embrace.

D. FEEDBACK AND RENEWAL SYSTEMS

Organizations have life cycles just as human do. One of the big differences, however, is that organizations can "renew" and rebuild themselves into completely different organizations, starting all over again. Phase B, Feedback Loop (from the environment) is a crucial variable at the start of this process. So is having a new future vision (Phase A) to act as a magnet, directing everyone forward to the "renewed" organization.

➦ For Example

A good example of large-scale renewal is what Jack Welch has done at General Electric. Another is IBM, which is well on its way to becoming a brand-new company as a systems service provider (while keeping its old company as a mainframe manufacturer). Being a learning organization and using environmental scanning and feedback are the keys to this.

Remember that . . .

> **Learning organizations cultivate the art of open, attentive listening. Managers must be open to criticism.**

Renewal Practices Questionnaire

The following questionnaire lists 35 practices that contribute to and support organizational renewal. Which of them can be found in your organization?

		QUESTIONNAIRE: RENEWAL PRACTICES

Directions: Do you have the following practices in your organization? Answer yes or no for each practice. When you are finished, go back and circle the practices you need to initiate.

Yes	No	RENEWAL PRACTICES
❑	❑	1. Issues-management process (government, community, stakeholders)
❑	❑	2. Environmental scanning system
❑	❑	3. Competitor analysis
❑	❑	4. Financial reports (short-term and long-term)
❑	❑	5. Industry financial comparisons
❑	❑	6. Customer data, surveys, feedback, perceptions, focus group
❑	❑	7. Non-customer data, surveys, perceptions, focus group
❑	❑	8. Observation of technological trends
❑	❑	9. Observation of socio-demographic trends
❑	❑	10. Rewards—matching surveys, programs, diagnosis

(Continued)

			QUESTIONNAIRE: RENEWAL PRACTICES *(continued)*

Yes	No		RENEWAL PRACTICES
❏	❏	11.	Employee-opinion surveys (morale, motivation, communication)—annually, by unit
❏	❏	12.	Culture surveys, focus groups
❏	❏	13.	Administrative MIS reports
❏	❏	14.	Action, research
❏	❏	15.	Advertising, marketing ROI and research
❏	❏	16.	Management date, opinions
❏	❏	17.	Task forces, think tanks, discussion groups
❏	❏	18.	Strategic-planning process
❏	❏	19.	Unfiltered upward-feedback meetings
❏	❏	20.	Team building, diagnosis, executive retreats
❏	❏	21.	Structured experiences, feedback and learning
❏	❏	22.	Job design, work simplifications
❏	❏	23.	Organization-effectiveness-suggestion programs (not just productivity)
❏	❏	24.	Employee-involvement programs
❏	❏	25.	Peer evaluations
❏	❏	26.	Meeting evaluations
❏	❏	27.	Employee-management meetings
❏	❏	28.	Offsite meetings, overnights, Outward Bound team experience
❏	❏	29.	Performance evaluations, including company values
❏	❏	30.	MBWA

(Continued)

QUESTIONNAIRE: RENEWAL PRACTICES *(concluded)*		
Yes	**No**	**RENEWAL PRACTICES**
☐	☐	31. Feedback, feedback, feedback
☐	☐	32. Deep-sensing employee perceptions
☐	☐	33. Best-practices research
☐	☐	34. Benchmarking
☐	☐	35. Work-flow mapping

E. STRATEGIC EDUCATION MODEL

Real learning in an organization requires knowledge
and skills, as well as the right attitude. And to affect
organizational change, it must move up from the individual
to teams and to the organization as a whole. These levels
are essential to creating a learning organization.

Exercise: Strategic Model
Place an *H, M,* or *L* in
each box to show the
levels of learning going
on for either (1) you,
(2) your department, or
(3) your organization
as a whole.

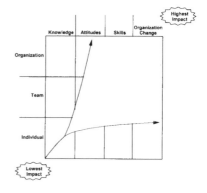

APPLICATIONS

V. The A-B-C-D Systems Model

The tools in this chapter are designed to increase your success with a number of key management processes and activities. They will help you apply the A-B-C-D Systems Model within the practical dimensions of the workplace.

TOOL NO.	THE APPLICATIONS
17.	"Organization as a System" Model*
18.	Reinventing Strategic Management
19.	Strategic Life Planning
20.	HR Strategic Planning
21.	Systemic Team Building
22.	Leadership Development as a System
23.	Hiring and Promotion as a System
➡ These Tools Will Help You with Key Management Processes!	

*Essential reading for all the tools in this chapter.

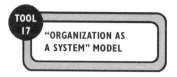

Application of
Standard Systems Dynamics
— 1. Holism
— 4. Input-Output
—10. Interrelated Parts

In this tool, we will focus on a primary application of the third concept of systems thinking—the A-B-C-D Systems Model. In Chapter I, we took an in-depth look at this model as an overall systems concept. Here we will discuss it as an application to the organization as a system—as a way to create *alignment* and *attunement* for the organization's competitive edge.

Refer to the close-up section below whenever necessary, to ensure you fully understand the "Organization as a System" Model (for a graphic depiction of the model, see Figure 8). As was noted earlier, this is essential reading for the other tools in this chapter, all of which are based on this model.

CLOSE-UP: "ORGANIZATION AS A SYSTEM" MODEL

Phase A: Customer Value (Output)

Systems thinking "begins with the end in mind," to borrow a phrase from Stephen Covey. *Outcomes, purposes, missions, visions, goals, objectives,* and *ends* are all terms that describe Phase A, the outcome of the organization as a system (also defined as *the customer edge*). The vital move here is to define who your customers are and what they want, and then to position the organization so it has a unique edge over the competition. This is the first and foremost strategic and systems thinking task any organization must invest its efforts in.

FIGURE 8. "ORGANIZATION AS A SYSTEM" MODEL

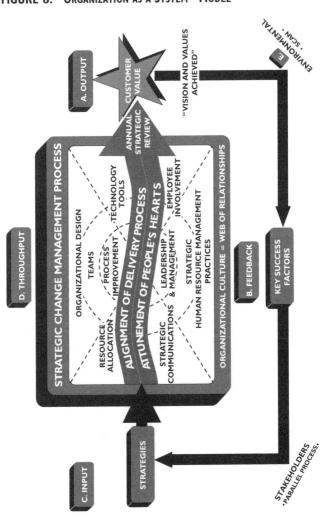

Obviously, to satisfy customer needs and thus achieve the desired outcomes, an organization must deal with a dynamic, changing environment. Good strategic thinking helps the organization look at future environmental trends to define where it wants to be within the context of that environment.

Phase B: Key Success Factors (Feedback Loop)

Phase B corresponds to the feedback loop, or in organizational terms, the key success factors. These factors are *the quantifiable outcome measures of success* and should be constantly fed back to the organization. (They are sometimes called goals and objectives.) Feeding back quantifiable measurements of how the organization is functioning *is essential to organizational learning.* It guides corrections and adjustments throughout the year to ensure achievement of Phase A, Customer Value.

Whether you describe this phase in terms of objectives, goals, key success indicators, critical success factors, or the like, it is all about *building a scoreboard of organizational-success measurements* and feeding the status of these back into the organization so it can learn from them and correct its actions as necessary.

Phase C: Strategies (Input)

This is where inputs into the organization as a system deal with creating the strategic edge. The 64-million-dollar question for organizations is "What core strategies do we need to adopt?" These strategies are crucial, for they are *the primary means to our ends of achieving organizational outcomes, especially customer value.* They represent strategic thinking at its very best.

Phase C includes the conversion of strategic plans into business plans and operational or annual department plans for each aspect of the organization. *The operational or annual department plans are what you implement*—not the strategic plans. A strategic plan is a blueprint and living, breathing document—a framework for creating business and operational plans. Thus Phase C inputs are crucial in *defining* the core strategies and, through conversion, the operational plans for implementing change throughout the organization.

Note that the Phase C tools in this chapter show all the aspects of strategic planning that lead to developing these core strategies. I have focused the material in this way, describing it in one place, for reasons of coherence. Technically, however, strategic planning includes parts of the other three phases—A, B, and C—as well.

Phase D: Strategic Change Management Process (Throughput)

The throughput of the organization as a system has to react to today's dynamic organizational changes. This phase details the inner workings of the organization in terms of systems and horizontal interdependent process (much as TQM and reengineering does), rather than by using the separate "functional boxes" so common in analytic organizational charts. It has four main components:

1. **Strategic change management process**
2. **Alignment of delivery processes**
3. **Attunement of people's hearts**
4. **The web of relationships**

The master component is putting in place a **strategic change management process.** It is the overall guiding leadership and management mechanism to assure that integrated and systemic change occurs. Instrumental to that success are the tasks of defining and putting in place *the change processes and structures.*

The second major component deals with the operational or technical part of Phase D throughputs—*creating the process edge*. This is done through **the alignment of the delivery processes** of the organization. In Figure 8, our model's alignment component is depicted not as a straight line, but as a wavy one, for in effect it occurs more in keeping with the Rollercoaster of Change (systems concept 4). It is half of **the web of relationships** (the fourth component, which strongly influences effective or ineffective delivery processes) and includes the five elements of organizational design, resource allocation, teams, process improvement, and technology tools. Note that most change efforts focus on this more operational or technical component (often to the detriment of the organization).

The third major component, **attunement of people's hearts** (and minds)**,** is crucial to creating customer value— *the people edge*. It is also the other half of **the web of relationships**, which ultimately creates your organizational culture.

For purposes of explanation, I have separated the social (the attunement of people's hearts) from the technical or operational (the alignment of the delivery processes); however, both are inextricably combined in Phase D as the organization's internal **web of relationships** that must integrate well and fit together in support of creating customer value (Phase A). Without integration and fit, we not only lack the synergy of 2 plus 2 equals 5, but face the likelihood that elements in the attunement and alignment will work against each other. *Fit*—a word that should be used with caution when it comes to systems thinking—is only applicable here in the sense that the basic purpose of these components is to assist, and work in conjunction with, other components to help the entire organization create customer value.

We thus encounter (and must manage) a systemic phenomenon: that maximizing any functional department's effectiveness sub-optimizes the whole organization. We must always remember: *the whole is primary and the parts should only be optimized as a secondary consideration.*

GUIDELINES FOR USE

I. Based on extensive best-practices research, the broad utility of the "Organization as a System" Model includes its use as:

   1. A template, model, or diagnostic tool

   2. A framework for thinking and analyzing the organization (or a department)

   3. A source of questions as you make decisions to change items or tasks in the organization (i.e., implement your strategic plan)

   4. A common framework for thinking, communicating, and working together to change parts of the organization and achieve your vision

   5. A way to increase awareness, sensitivity, and understanding of how an organization works and how the parts should fit together in support of vision/customers

   6. A way to eliminate biases

   7. A tool for gaining focus despite organizational complexity

   8. A tool to diagnose the status of your effectiveness in achieving the organization's fit, alignment, and integrity with regard to your vision and your desired culture

   9. An exquisitely simple macro model for getting a handle on organizational changes

   10. A bird's-eye view/framework for looking at the overall organization

       • To see multiple cause and effect

       • To find a balanced way to "cover the waterfront"

   11. An aid for narrowing in on areas needing work

       • To set priorities for work

       • To see clear linkages/interdependence to other functions, tasks

(Continued)

GUIDELINES FOR USE
(Concluded)

12. A road map—a way not to get lost in organization complexity

    • To know where you are and how to navigate toward success

    • To have a 21st-century road map, not a 1700s one

13. A tool to diagnose problems/solutions in organizations; a way to increase the chance of success by seeing how one thing affects all others (vital when you're attempting culture change)

14. A method for explaining and teaching executives/managers how to manage and lead strategic planning and change; as a readiness check

15. A guide for large-scale change and for improving individual/team performance and links to vision/values and direction

16. A way to gain more confidence in your implementation

17. A view of how multi-causes have multi-effects

    • Simple cause-effect is obsolete

18. Help to avoid strategies/actions based on a systems diagnosis and "solid" solutions

See the helpful, best-practices diagnostic tool on the following page.

2. **Use the organization system model to conduct a high-performance survey and assessment on the status of the components and their interrelationships. See the survey that closes this tool.**

BEST-PRACTICES RESEARCH *A Diagnostic Tool for Managing Accelerated Change*				
PHASES	**Organization Type ▶▶** **Organization ⤴ as a System**	**A.** **REACTIVE ORGANIZATION**	**B.** *Industrial Age* **RESPONSIBLE ORGANIZATION** (Traditional)	**C.** *Systems Age* **HIGH-PERF. ORGANIZATION** (Proactive)
A. **Output**	1. Achievement of Results	Survival Level & Conflict Only	Profitability OK or Within Budget	Customer Value (★ Results)
B. **Feedback**	2. Feedback Loop	Rarely Used (Closed System)	Financial/Operational Measures Only	KSFs/Annual Strategic Review/ Org. Learning
A.–C. **Strategic Planning**	3. Strategic Planning	Survival/Confusion Day to Day	3-Year Forecasts/ Operational Planning	Integrate Strategic Mgmt. System
D. **Alignment** **(of Delivery Processes)**	4A. Operational Tasks (Quality/Service) 4B. Technology 4C. Resources 4D. Organizational Design 4E. Team Development 4F. Business Processes	A. Firefighting/Fix It (Low Quality) B. Out of Date C. Squeaky Wheel D. Fragmented E. Adversarial/ Individ. Focus F. Personal Control	A. Maintain Only/ Obsolete Tasks B. Piecemeal Technology C. Incrementalism D. Hierarchy & Bureaucracy E. Functional Teams Only F. Bureaucratic/ Department Controls	A. Reputation for High-Quality/Service B. Technology Fit/ Organization C. Resources on Clear Focus D. Networks/Flat Strategic Alliances E. Cross-Funct'l, Self-Managed F. Customer-Focused (Value Chain)
D. **Attune-ment (of People's Hearts)**	5A. Leadership & Mgmt. 5B. Employee Involvement	A. Enforcing Blaming (Incompetence) B. Avoid Blame/Wait	A. Directing/Controlling B. Obedient Doers	A. Six Competencies (All System Levels B. Empowered

(Continued)

		A.	B.	C.
BEST-PRACTICES RESEARCH *A Diagnostic Tool for Managing Accelerated Change*				
PHASES	**Organization Type ➡** _____ **Organization ↖ as a System**	**REACTIVE ORGANIZATION**	*Industrial Age* **RESPONSIBLE ORGANIZATION** (Traditional)	*Systems Age* **HIGH-PERF. ORGANIZATION** (Proactive)
D. Attune- ment (of People's Hearts)	5C. Strategic Communications 5D. Human Resources 5E. Culture Change	C. Minimal/Negative D. Poor People Management E. One Man Rule	C. Formal Newsletter D. Low Risk E. Command & Control	C. Strategic Positive/Open Book D. Empower Employees to Serve Customer E. Participative Leadership (Facilitate & Support)
E. Strategic Change Mgmt. Process	6. Strategic Change Management	Avoid Pain Only (No Follow-Through)	Isolated Change Projects	Transformational Change—Proactive
	7. Annual Strategic Review	Not on Radar Scope	Department Goals & Objectives	Strategic Plan— Living, Breathing Updated Document

Notice the Paradigm Shift from the Industrial Age, Traditional Organization to the Systems Age, Proactive Organization

HIGH-PERFORMANCE ORGANIZATION SURVEY

Directions: (1) Circle the number that best describes your organization as it is today. Total your score.
(2) Connect the circles with a vertical line. The resulting zigzag shows where your organization's emphasis has been (high #s) and not been (low #s). The zigzag's extent is the extent of lack of congruence and fit of these parts of your organization with its outputs.

	REACTIVE ORG. A				RESPONSIBLE ORG. B				HIGH-PERF. ORG. C	
A. Output											
1. Achievement of Results	1	2	3	4	5	6	7	8	9	10	
B. Feedback											
2. Feedback Loop	1	2	3	4	5	6	7	8	9	10	
A–C Strategic Planning											
3. Strategic Planning	1	2	3	4	5	6	7	8	9	10	
D. Alignment—Delivery											
4A. Operational Tasks (Quality Service)	1	2	3	4	5	6	7	8	9	10	
4B. Technology	1	2	3	4	5	6	7	8	9	10	
4C. Resources	1	2	3	4	5	6	7	8	9	10	
4D. Organizational Design	1	2	3	4	5	6	7	8	9	10	
4E. Team Development	1	2	3	4	5	6	7	8	9	10	
4F. Business Processes	1	2	3	4	5	6	7	8	9	10	
D. Attunement—People											
5A. Leadership & Management	1	2	3	4	5	6	7	8	9	10	
5B. Employee Involvement	1	2	3	4	5	6	7	8	9	10	
5C. Strategic Communications	1	2	3	4	5	6	7	8	9	10	
5D. Human Resources	1	2	3	4	5	6	7	8	9	10	
5E. Culture Change	1	2	3	4	5	6	7	8	9	10	
D. Strat. Change Mgmt. Proc.											
6. Strategic Change Management	1	2	3	4	5	6	7	8	9	10	
7. Annual Strategic Review	1	2	3	4	5	6	7	8	9	10	

(Continued)

HIGH-PERFORMANCE ORGANIZATION SURVEY

Scoring:

TOTAL SCORE = _____ (160 points possible)

A. High-Performing Organization = 110 to 160 points
B. Responsible Organization = 60 to 110 points
C. Reactive Organization = 0 to 60 points

Comments on Survey Responses/Results:

TOOL 18 REINVENTING STRATEGIC MANAGEMENT

Application of
The A-B-C-D
Systems Model

Reinvented strategic management, a process from the
Centre for Strategic Management, is a different way to
apply systems thinking and the A-B-C-D framework. Use it
to tailor and build various strategic planning processes and
integrate them right into strategic change. The details of
the process model are shown in Figure 9, on the next page.

The process model illustrates there are many uses of the
four phases of systems thinking.

A. Creating your ideal future (Output)
B. Measuring success (Feedback Loop)
C. Converting strategies to operations (Input, to action)
D. Achieving successful implementation (Throughput,
   action) And scanning the environment on a
   continuous basis

➡️ **For Example**

Potential applications of this process include:

1. **Comprehensive Strategic Plan**, to do a
   comprehensive strategic planning process for an
   entire organization. Requires 10 to 16 days offsite;
   full steps 1 to 10, yet tailored to the organization.
   (Explaining this full process is beyond our scope
   here; for more information and a four-page summary
   article about it, contact the Centre for Strategic
   Management at 619-275-6528.)

2. **Strategic Planning Quick**, to conduct a shortened
   and less comprehensive version of strategic planning
   for an entire organization. This requires five days

FIGURE 9. PROCESS: REINVENTING STRATEGIC MANAGEMENT

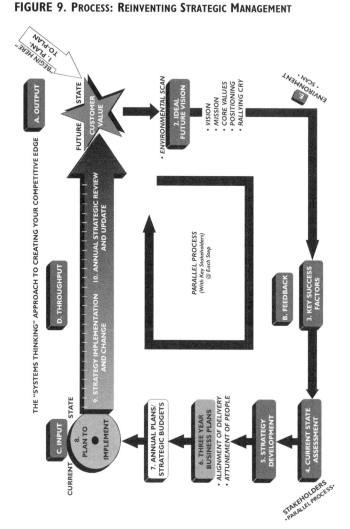

offsite. (See the "plan quick" version of the process model, later in this tool.)

3. **Business/Functional Strategic Planning**, to conduct a shortened three-year business planning process for a line business unit or major support function/section/program (i.e., element of the larger organization). Requires 5 to 10 days, depending on if a comprehensive strategic plan (no. 1 above) is first accomplished. (See process model, this tool.)

4. **Micro Strategic Planning**, to develop a strategic plan for a small organization or business. Requires two days offsite; do the rest without meetings. (See process model, this tool.)

5. **Strategic Life Plan**, to conduct a personal (person, family, couple) life plan. (Use with Tool 19.)

6. **Strategic Human Resource Management**, to create *"the people edge"* in your organization. (Use with Tool 20.)

7. **Leadership Development System**, to enhance your leadership roles and competencies as a competitive business edge. (Use with Tool 22.)

8. **Organizational Systems Model**, to systematically diagnose any change effort and dramatically increase your probability of success. (Use in conjunction with Tool 17.)

9. **Team Effectiveness**, to comprehensively focus on all aspects of teams to dramatically enhance their outcomes and effectiveness. (Use with Tool 21.)

> **Be sure to go beyond planning into strategic change with each use!**

Tailoring and Rating Sheet

Complete the following tailoring and rating sheet, basing your ratings on your current understanding of reinventing strategic planning, using your organization as a model.

REINVENTING STRATEGIC PLANNING: TAILORING AND RATING SHEET

Directions: How important is it for your organization to develop the deliverables below? Rate each one's importance from high (H) to medium (M) to low (L).

H — M — L **POTENTIAL DELIVERABLES**

Strategic Planning—Stage 2 to 5

H	M	L		
❑	❑	❑	1. Environmental Scanning (SKEPTIC)	
❑	❑	❑	2. Vision	
❑	❑	❑	3. Mission	**A**
❑	❑	❑	4. Values	
❑	❑	❑	5. Driving Forces	
❑	❑	❑	5a. Rallying Cry	
❑	❑	❑	6. Key Success Factors	**B**
❑	❑	❑	7. Current State Assessment	
❑	❑	❑	7a. Scenario/Contingency Planning	
❑	❑	❑	8. Core Strategies/Actions/Yearly Priorities	

Business Units—Stage 6

H	M	L		
❑	❑	❑	9. SBU/MPAs Defined	
❑	❑	❑	9a. Business/Key Support Plans (3-Year Mini-Strategic Plans)	

Annual Plans—Stage 7

H	M	L		
❑	❑	❑	10. Annual Plans/Priorities/Department Plans	
❑	❑	❑	11. Resource Allocation/Budgeting (including guidelines)	**C**

Individuals/Teams

H	M	L		
❑	❑	❑	12. Individual Performance Management System —Tied to Strategic Planning	
❑	❑	❑	12a. Rewards & Recognition System —Tied to Strategic Planning	

Bridge the Gap—Step 8

H	M	L		
❑	❑	❑	13. Plan-to-Implement Day	

(Continued)

REINVENTING STRATEGIC PLANNING: TAILORING AND RATING SHEET
(Continued)

H — M — L			POTENTIAL DELIVERABLES

Focus on the Vital Four (★ Results)—Align Delivery—Step 9

H	M	L		
❑	❑	❑	14a.	Quality Products and Services
❑	❑	❑	14b.	Customer Service
❑	❑	❑	14c.	Organization Structure/Redesign
❑	❑	❑	14d.	Business Process Reengineering (BPR) to lower costs & improve customer response (customer focused)
❑	❑	❑	14e.	Blow Out Bureaucracy (& Waste)
❑	❑	❑	14f.	Speed/Responsiveness

Management Development—Attunement of People/Support Systems—Step 9

H	M	L		
❑	❑	❑	15a.	Professional Management and Leadership Competencies, Skills, & Practices Workshop (trainer, coach, facilitator)
❑	❑	❑	15b.	Skills Built Through the Managing Strategic Change Workshop
❑	❑	❑	15c.	HR Programs/Processes (E.D.C.)
❑	❑	❑	15d.	Values/Cultural Change
❑	❑	❑	15e.	Strategic Budgeting
❑	❑	❑	15f.	Information Technology (T.S.G.)

Yearly Update—Step 10

H	M	L		
❑	❑	❑	16.	Annual Strategic Review & Update
❑	❑	❑	17a.	Teamwork for Executive Team
❑	❑	❑	17b.	Teamwork for Department Teams
❑	❑	❑	17c.	Teamwork for Cross-Functional Relationships/Teams

D

Strategic Planning Quick

For a quick-planning variant of reinvented strategic management, see the process shown in Figure 10, on the following page.

Three-Year Business Planning or Mini-Strategic Planning

There are three major steps to this kind of planning. The steps listed below should be taken for *all strategic business units and major organizational support units.*

Step 1: Create Your Ideal Future Vision
- Duration—two days
- Conduct educational briefing and Plan-to-Plan or Corporate Strategic Plan review.
- Refine or develop your vision, mission, and values in draft form (Step 2 of SPQ model), using Corporate's as a guide.
- Develop Corporate goals with outcome measures of success (alternative).
- Develop key-stakeholder parallel process.

Step 2: Convert Strategies to Operations
- Duration—two days
- Finalize your ideal future vision (Step 2).
- Conduct current state assessment (Step 4).
- Develop your core strategies (Step 5) and top-priority action items for the next year—the "glue."
- Set up second key-stakeholder feedback.

Step 3: Strategy Implementation and Change
- Duration—at first, one day every two months
- First set of tasks: finalize core strategies and actions (Steps 5 and 7).
- Set up quarterly meeting of the Strategic Change Leadership Steering Committee (Step 9) to maintain plan success and/or decide on SBUs (Step 6).
- Conduct Plan-to-Implement (Step 8).

FIGURE 10. Strategic Planning Quick Process

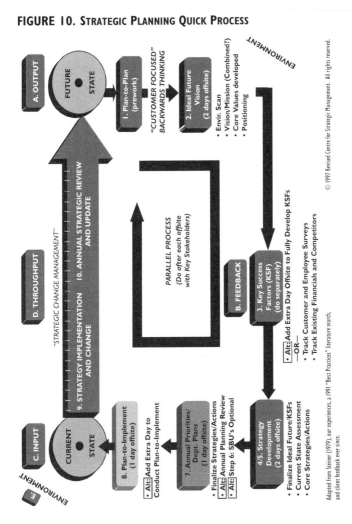

Adapted from Steiner (1979), our experiences, a 1991 "Best Practices" literature search, and client feedback ever since.

Note on Feedback Loop: *Key success factors (Step 3) are not recommended due to time limits;* ***instead,*** *monitor core strategies and existing financials; survey customers and employees.*

"Micro" Strategic Planning, for Smaller Organizations

Step 1: **Create Your Ideal Future Vision** (one-day offsite)
- Conduct educational briefing and Plan-to-Plan before the offsite. (Include key-stakeholder parallel process.)
- Refine or develop your vision, mission, and values in draft form (Step 2 of SPQ model).
- Develop a "key success factor" process outside the offsites.
- Set up a current state assessment to be accomplished between Steps 1 and 2.

Step 2: **Plan-to-Implement Your Future Successfully** (one-day offsite)
- Finalize your ideal future vision (Step 2).
- Present/Review current state assessment (Step 4).
- Develop core strategies (Step 5) and action items.
- Set up annual planning/budget process to follow this micro strategic planning.

Step 3: **Strategy Implementation and Change** (one-day offsite)
- First set of tasks: finalize core strategies and annual plans (Steps 5 and 7).
- Set up quarterly meeting of Strategic Change Leadership Steering Committee (Step 9) to maintain plan's success; decide on SBUs (Step 6); conduct Plan-to-Implement (Step 8).

Note on Feedback Loop: *KSFs (Step 3) are not recommended;* ***instead,*** *monitor core strategies and existing financials; survey customers and employees. Do this outside planning steps and offsites above; when completed, present to board / planning team for final approval.*

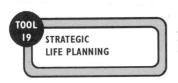

TOOL 19 · STRATEGIC LIFE PLANNING

Application of
• Seven Levels of Living Systems
• The A-B-C-D Systems Model

Look before, or you'll find yourself behind.

—Benjamin Franklin
(*Bartlett's Familiar Quotations,* 14th edition, 1968)

The clarity of an individual's search for meaning is important to the organization's success as well as the individual's. The better the match, the better the results organizationally and professionally. Thus managers need to help employees develop not only a career path but also *a strategic life plan* to stimulate employee initiative and focus their energy. The A-B-C-D framework is fully applicable to this goal, as shown in simplified form below and in more detail in Figure 12 (see next page).

FIGURE II. STRATEGIC LIFE PLANNING PROCESS—SIMPLIFIED FORM

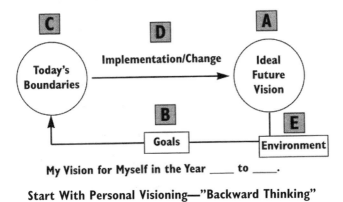

My Vision for Myself in the Year ____ to ____.

Start With Personal Visioning—"Backward Thinking"

FIGURE 12. STRATEGIC LIFE PLANNING PROCESS

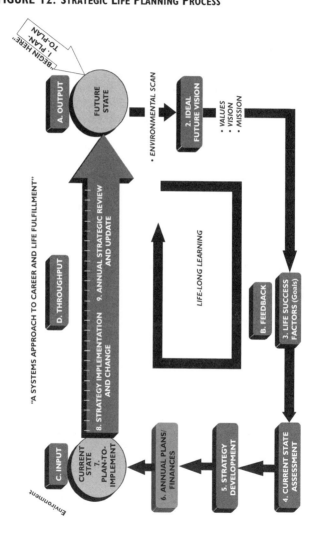

Exercises: Personal Vision and Personal Values

Use the following worksheets to begin putting strategic life planning into practice, and to work, in *your* life.

WORKSHEET I: PERSONAL VISION EXERCISE		

1. Brainstorm your personal vision; then ask: "How will I know I have achieved my vision?" Provide answers, using the chart below.

ROLES	VISION	MEASURES OF SUCCESS AT YEAR _____
PERSONAL		
1. Physical Health		
2. Mental/Learning		
3. Emotional/Spiritual (Ethical)		
FINANCIAL		
4. Lifestyle/Wealth		
PROFESSIONAL		
5. Job/Career		
INTERPERSONAL		
6. Social/Friends		
7. Community/ Service		
8. Immediate Family (Home, Spouse)		
9. Extended Family (Parents, Siblings)		

2. Now try to get your vision down to a single statement. Also, think of what your "rallying cry" should be, putting it into eight words or less.

(Continued)

WORKSHEET 11: PERSONAL VALUES EXERCISE

Rank the following values from 1 to 15, with 1 being the most important to you and 15 being the least important.

VALUES	ACTUAL	DESIRED
1. Having good relationships with colleagues		
2. Professional reputation/respect		
3. Achievement of organization/unit goals		
4. Teamwork and collaboration		
5. Leisure time for enjoyment/fun		
6. Wealth and prosperity		
7. Fitness and health		
8. Contribution, service to society, community		
9. Acknowledging others' achievements		
10. Autonomy/Freedom to act		
11. Personal growth		
12. Time with family/close friends		
13. Ethical behavior		
14. Excitement and challenge		
15. Spiritual/Religious time		

NOTE: If a person's vision and values don't match the organization's, you have *a motivation gap*. Identify such gaps and deal with them personally and organizationally.

Application of
• Seven Levels of Living Systems
• Standard Systems Dynamics
  — 4. Input-Output
• The A-B-C-D Systems Model

This tool presents a systems approach to creating an HR strategic plan by combining the A-B-C-D framework with strategic HR areas. A planning model is shown below; an HR management model is provided later in the tool.

FIGURE 13. HR STRATEGIC PLANNING MODEL

Human Resource Strategic Planning

The People System to Create a High-Performance Organization

Using HR Strategic Planning

The steps for HR strategic planning are the same as those for organizational strategic planning; however, in this case, you do the planning for the HR function or department, not the entire organization. The steps are ordered in accordance with the A-B-C-D framework, as shown below.

Step A: **Future State**
- Conduct educational briefing and Plan-to-Plan on entire process.
- Link to organizational vision, mission, values, strategy.
- Ensure senior management commitment to the process and its outcomes.
- Define Human Resource ideal future vision.
- Develop clear HR systems model/framework. (Use A-B-C-D framework; see Figure 14 for guidance.)

Step B: **Feedback Loop**
- Use HR information systems/HR key success factors based on the HR Systems Model.
- Set HR standards, measures.
- Use surveys to measure them.
- Use rewards system for HR plan achievement.
- Get stakeholder involvement and input.

Step C: **Current State**
- Conduct organizational diagnosis on HR system's effectiveness along with its fit with the other tracks.
- Develop strategic action items to support the plan.
- Ensure HR Strategic Plan includes a consideration of all aspects of the HR Systems Model, including:
  — Succession/manpower planning
  — Career development
  — Hiring, assimilation, start-up
  — ER/HR policies
  — Union/management relations

  — Organization/management development
    system
  — Training, education system, programs
  — Performance/Rewards management
  — Compensation and benefits
  — EEO/Wellness/QWL
  — Internal communications systems
  — Job/Organization design and descriptions
  — HR MIS
- Provide resource allocation to support the desired
  changes.

Step D: Strategy Implementation and Change—Major Activities
- Educate management on HR systems and
  organizational behavior.
- Roll out/Communicate the HR strategic plan.
- Become steward, and maintain stewardship, of
  the HR strategic plan, organizational culture,
  values.
- Ensure fit/integration/coordination with any other
  major improvement processes (i.e., systems fit—
  alignment and integrity).

Human Resource as a System: The Human Resource Management Systems Model

Are all of your HR programs and processes linked to your
organization's strategic plan, especially its vision, values
and strategies? To ensure this linkage, use the Strategic
Human Resource Management (HRM) Systems Model,
shown in Figure 14, on the next page. This model will help
you gain the crucial "people edge"—a system of people flow
and movement over time.

The HRM Systems Model is followed by a comprehensive
list of HR practices and programs that will give you a hand
with assessing your "people edge" (see Figure 15).

FIGURE 14. STRATEGIC HUMAN RESOURCE MANAGEMENT SYSTEMS MODEL

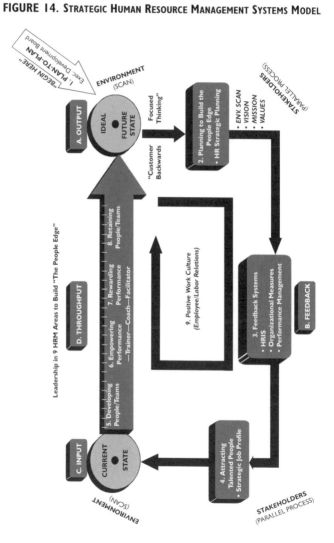

FIGURE 15. STRATEGIC HRM SYSTEMS MODEL: DETAILS

9 AREAS AND 36 KEY HRM PROCESSES TO ENSURE "THE PEOPLE EDGE"

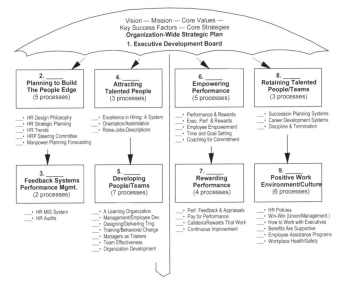

Vision — Mission — Core Values —
Key Success Factors — Core Strategies
Organization-Wide Strategic Plan
1. Executive Development Board

2. _____ Planning to Build The People Edge (5 processes)	4. _____ Attracting Talented People (3 processes)	6. _____ Empowering Performance (5 processes)	8. _____ Retaining Talented People/Teams (3 processes)
___• HR Design Philosophy	___• Excellence in Hiring: A System	___• Performance & Rewards	___• Succession Planning Systems
___• HR Strategic Planning	___• Orientation/Assimilation	___• Exec. Perf. & Rewards	___• Career Development Systems
___• HR Trends	___• Roles-Jobs-Descriptions	___• Employee Empowerment	___• Discipline & Termination
___• HRP Steering Committee		___• Time and Goal Setting	
___• Manpower Planning Forecasting		___• Coaching for Commitment	

3. _____ Feedback Systems Performance Mgmt. (2 processes)	5. _____ Developing People/Teams (7 processes)	7. _____ Rewarding Performance (4 processes)	9. _____ Positive Work Environment/Culture (6 processes)
___• HR MIS System	___• A Learning Organization	___• Perf. Feedback & Appraisals	___• HR Policies
___• HR Audits	___• Management/Employee Dev.	___• Pay for Performance	___• Win-Win (Union/Management.)
	___• Designing/Delivering Trng.	___• Cafeteria Rewards That Work	___• How to Work with Executives
	___• Training/Behavioral Change	___• Continuous Improvement	___• Benefits Are Supportive
	___• Managers as Trainers		___• Employee Assistance Programs
	___• Team Effectiveness.		___• Workplace Health/Safety
	___• Organization Development		

GUIDELINES FOR USE

1. Use the detailed list in Figure 15 to do a comprehensive assessment of your organization's "people practices."

2. After the comprehensive assessment, use the Strategic HRM Systems Model as part of your HR strategic planning process. The model will provide you with clear clues to the strategies you need to implement.

Application of
- Standard Systems Dynamics
  — 4. Input-Output
- The A-B-C-D Systems Model

Systems thinking is *the* method for problem solving and team building. The systems approach to team building is shown below in Figure 16. Here are the steps:

Step 1: *Phase A.* Define the idea state in the future.
Step 2: *Phase B.* Develop feedback mechanisms and norms for people to learn and grow as individuals or as a team.
Step 3: *Phase C.* Diagnose where we are now.
Step 4: Action-plan how to get from today *(C)* to future *(A)*.

Make your team building and development more systemic, thorough, and long-lasting by using the A-B-D-C systems framework.

FIGURE 16. SYSTEMS APPROACH TO TEAM-BUILDING

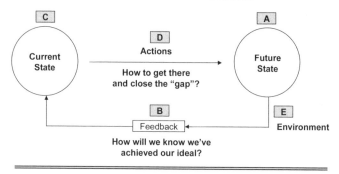

Developing High-Performance Teams

High-performance teams are the way to run the business. Needed is team development of all types and at all levels of the organization. The actions below, if taken in the order presented, will lead to such development.

A. Future State
- Conduct education briefing and Plan-to-Plan on entire process.
- Ensure senior management's commitment and willingness to undergo personal growth and guided self-change.
- Clarify ideal future vision for teams.
- Develop clarity on levels and types of teams desired (by priority); for example, project teams, functional teams, cross-functional teams, self-managed teams.
- Link to organizational vision, mission, and values.

B. Feedback Loop
- Team standards and inter/intra-team feedback.
- Stakeholder involvement and input.
- Follow-up/reinforcement systems in place.
- Continual improvement/renewal philosophy in place.
- Rewards systems to reinforce desired changes.
- Best practices research.

C. Current State
- Conduct a team diagnosis of each team and its fit with the other tracks.
- Develop strategic action items to support the plans for team development.
- Provide resource allocation to support desired changes.

D. Strategy Implementation and Change—Major Activities
- Ensure education and understanding of the team development model.
- Conduct team-building process for teams selected with regular follow-up check points.

- Learn skills in:
  - Meetings management and role clarification
  - Group dynamics, process, and facilitation
  - Team leadership and management functions
  - Interpersonal and influence management, as well as communications
  - Ethical persuasion, decision making, and conflict resolution
- Develop a proactive management fit and coordination with outside sources of impact, the other tracks, and any other major improvement projects (i.e., systems fit, alignment, and integrity).

Team-Building Effectiveness

Effective team-building is accomplished by the A-B-C-D Phases as shown in Figure 16. Each phase and its accompanying actions are explained below.

Phase I—Data Gathering and Data Analysis/Synthesis
- Personal interviews/other methods
- Observation on the job and studying records
- Requires time to gather input from other specialists and people with relevant information on team.
- Necessitates time by consultant to collate data into summary report.
- Preparation of client (team leader) for offsite meeting

Phase II—Offsite Meeting
- Definition of *A* (clear future vision).
- How will we know we are there? *(B)*
- Presentation of findings in summary report *(C)*
  - Exactly that—what we looked for, what we found
  - Assimilation/analysis of data—what it means
  - Problem identification, action planning
- Decisions/Action planning

FIGURE 17. EFFECTIVE TEAM BUILDING

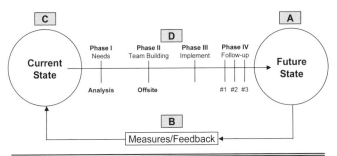

— Given the implications of being at **C** and desiring to
be at **A**, what needs to happen to get there? **(D)**

— Result: Plan of specific actions that need to occur, in
what order, involving how many people, by when

Phase III—Implementation of Action Plan (*D*)

• Accomplish task (i.e., achieve goals).

• Begin to build independence from consultant; do self-
diagnosis of your team effectiveness on an ongoing basis.

Phase IV—Monitoring/Follow-Up (Feedback Loop = *B*)

• Minimum of two half-day team meetings with consultant
within four to six weeks of, and within three months
following, first offsite meeting in order to assess results
to date and further actions needed; can be on site or off
site as needed.

• Consultant makes periodic visits to staff meetings as
process consultant.

• Consultant works with designated person to monitor
progress of action plan developed at first offsite meeting.

• Involvement of consultant in action steps as appropriate.

TOOL
22

LEADERSHIP
DEVELOPMENT
AS A SYSTEM

Application of
• Standard Systems Dynamics
— 4. Input-Output

*If we know one thing today, . . . it is most managers are
made, not born. . . . There has to be systematic work on the
supply, the development, and the skills of tomorrow's
management. . . . It cannot be left to change.*

—Peter F. Drucker (Tarraut, 1976)

Thinking of leadership development as a system, instead of
just providing training programs, is an entirely new way of
thinking. Every leader and organization should think this
way, for when we boil competitive edges to their essence,
leaders and managers are the only true sustainable edge
over the long term. Thus using a system of development is
one of the best ways to gain and maintain this edge,
individual and collectively.

***Leadership practices are the ultimate competitive
advantage and the foundation for all else.***

➡ **For Example**

Leadership is needed at all organizational levels.
- Executive
- Managerial
- Supervisory
- Professional/Technical
- Team
- Operational

➡ **For Example**

Senior management defensiveness is one big barrier to
leadership development. This seems to be a common
problem in change programs, where managers reason
defensively and change becomes a mere fad. Change

has to start at the top, as defensive senior managers are likely to disown any transformation in behavior or pattern of reason coming from lower levels.

Control and Discipline Start With You as a Leader

He who knows much about others may be learned,
but he who understands himself is more intelligent.
He who controls others may be powerful,
but he who has mastered himself is mightier still.

—Lao Tsu, Tao Te Ching

System Concepts: Strategic Leadership Development

The system concepts below are essential to effective leadership development and gaining "the people edge." (A leadership development system model will follow.)

Core Concepts of Leadership

Set of core concepts . . .
- is the responsibility of senior management.
- is usually carried out and led through an executive/employee development board (an EDB).
- includes the concept of individual development plan.
- is tied to the strategic plan, especially strategies/values.

Alignment of People Process

The EDB's role is to align the following processes to the strategic plan in order to create "the people edge" at the executive and lower-management levels.
1. Selection/Hiring
2. Promotion/Succession planning
3. Executive development
4. Management development

5. Career development/Life planning
6. Rewards, both intrinsic and extrinsic

Individual Development Plan (IDP) Concept

This needs to cover at least three levels of management:
1. Executives
2. Middle management
3. First-line supervisors

Core Skills and Values

While the continuously changing environment creates the need for a living, breathing, flexible leadership development system, it also requires a set of core skills such as:

- Self-mastery
- Coaching and Counseling
- Learning how to learn; reflection time
- Training others/Mentoring them
- Facilitating groups and teams
- Handling disagreements constructively

It also requires valuing the following:

- Integrity
- Curiosity
- Discovery
- Dialogue

Building a Strategic Leadership Development System: Model

Our model is shown in Figure 18. Here are its details and focal considerations, in sequence:

I. Plan-to-Plan
- Hold executive briefing on leadership.
- Form leadership development board and support team.
- Review best-practices research on leadership.
- Tailor the strategic leadership development system to your needs.
- Make commitment to proceed.

(Note: As preparation for the above, you can read the Centre for Strategic Management's summary article on leadership; contact CSM at 619-275-6528 for details.)

FIGURE 18. LEADERSHIP DEVELOPMENT SYSTEM PROCESS

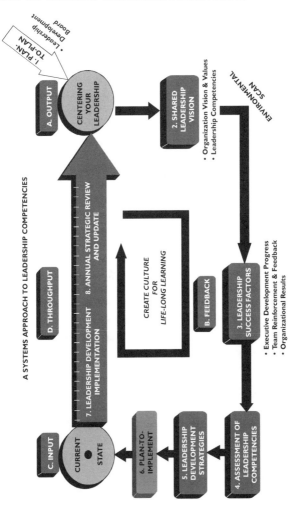

2. Shared Leadership Vision
- Clarify organizational vision, values, strategic plan.
- Establish leadership vision, principles, and mindsets tied to strategic plan.
- Tailor the leadership competencies/outcomes.

3. Reinforcement and Feedback Systems
- Leadership progress and success factors
- Best-practices benchmarks
- Create or refine feedback on leadership competencies

4. Assessment of Collective Leadership Competencies
- Self and others (360-degree)
- Competency maps
- Other tailored assessments—leadership styles, etc.

5. Leadership Development Strategies (and Actions)
- Master Personal Development Plan (PDP) inventory/format
- Modular development options
- Resources, timing, and reinforcement
- PDP administration and support structures
- Rewards, recognition, and succession planning tied to development
- Performance appraisal ties to strategic plan and development

6. Plan-to-Implement—Leadership Development Board
- Expectations
- Kick-off development
- Buddy system
- Develop coaching and mentoring skills

6A. Personal Development Plans
- Established for each executive, with individual priorities
- Individual skills assessment; leadership-styles instruments

- One to three years in length
- Clear sign off of authority

7. Implement Leadership Development
- Implementation of coaching and mentoring
- Sharing and spreading our learning
- Track, report, adjust . . .
  — quarterly reports
  — supervisor reviews
  — performance appraisal ties

8. Annual Leadership Review (and Update)
- Yearly revisions/updates

GUIDELINES FOR USE

I. Use this process to create a culture for life-long learning.
    A positive culture includes:
    - **Stairway of Learning**
    - **Supportive, challenging environment**
    - **Positive reinforcement**

    Remember key stakeholders and environmental scanning.
    This includes:
    - **Customers**
    - **Suppliers**
    - **Board of Directors**
    - **Employees**

2. For further information on this process, presented in a
    four-page article, call the Centre of Strategic Management
    at 619-275-6528.

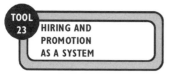

TOOL 23 HIRING AND PROMOTION AS A SYSTEM

Application of
• Standard Systems Dynamics
  — 9. Hierarchy
• The A-B-C-D Systems Model

Ensure every selection decision you make is successful. Take the guesswork out of selection each time and every time with the A-B-C-D systems approach shown below.

FIGURE 19. HIRING AND PROMOTION AS A SYSTEM

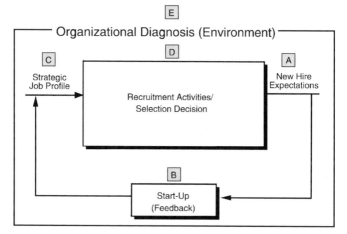

Phase A and D are notably important areas of the model. In this tool we'll take a look at these two phases, which involve, respectively (and in part), building a strategic job profile (SJP) and making the selection decision.

Focus on Phase A. Building The Strategic Job Profile (SJP)

This is the beginning of your search for the right person for the job. Start by defining your expectations of the new hire, *(Phase A)*, including job outcomes; then convert them to your strategic job profile. Use the profile as your input to drive decision-making (*Phase C*).

Here are some questions you will need to consider:
- What is the job title?
  Pay range/expected offer?
  Expected start date?
- What are the responsibilities and design of job?
- Other key jobs and reporting relationships (three-way: up, down, and sideways), and their fit with this job?
- Hiring manager's goals and expectations for this job?
- What is the supervisor's managerial style and personality?
- What are the initial priorities and tasks of this job?
- What challenges and problems are connected to this job?
- What resources are available (people, money, materials) to do the job?
- What qualifications (knowledge and experience) are required/preferred?
  (a) Required?
  (b) Preferred?
- What personal values are desired of the person for the job?
- What mix of skills is needed?

— Technical	_____
— Interpersonal	_____
— Managerial/Leadership	_____
— Conceptual/Strategic	_____
	= 100%

- What type of personality/communication style is desired? (For example, do you want someone who is expressive? amiable? analytical? driving?)

- How does this job fit in the life cycle of the organization?
- What organizational strategic thrust(s) must this person agree with and help implement?

Focus on Phase D. The Selection Decision Process

The selection process involves a number of tasks and considerations. Among them are the following:

1. Hold decision meetings.
2. Consider whether a quick decision will mean the right decision.
3. Make sure someone is responsible for reference checks. (Ask: "Whose responsibility are reference checks, back doors?")
4. Verify resumes, especially education section of them.
5. Hold informal interview to get to know the person. (Consider having dinner with him or her.)
6. Your strategic job profile should act as criteria.
7. Watch out for personal biases. (Do you have biases to overcome?)
8. Consider whether there are any reasons not to hire the person (if you "like" him or her).
9. Be aware that assertive people may be threatening or aggressive types after hire.
10. Be aware that friendly people are sometimes "wimps" after hire.

Selection Decision Matrix

When hiring for a key position in the organization, put two to four finalists into a "selection decision matrix" like the one on the following page. Then compare each finalist against your decision criteria. Note the use of the SJP in the selection decision matrix.

SELECTION DECISION MATRIX				
	FINALISTS SKILLS (H-M-L)			
STRATEGIC JOB PROFILE	1.	2.	3.	4.
1. Job Design 2. Roles (3-way) 3. Expectations, Goals				
4. Initial Priorities 5. Challenges, Problems 6. Resources Available				
7. Supervisor Style 8. Qualifications, Knowledge, Experience 9. Personality, Values				
10. Management Style 11. Mix of Skills: (a) Technical (b) Interpersonal (c) Mgmt./Leadership (d) Conceptual/Strats.				
12. Compensation, Promote Mediocrity 13. Employment Contracts				

GUIDELINES FOR USE

1. Note that successful hiring is most effectively done through the following best practices:
   - Multiple interviews
   - A group decision process
   - Comparing perspectives
   - Full references
   - Checking past success/behaviors as a guide to future success/behavior

2. This systems approach can be used for promotion as well. Add performance reviews and supervisory recommendations to your list of considerations. Also pay attention to the outcomes of the job the person now holds and the outcomes expected in the new position.

VI. Levels of Living Systems

The tools in this chapter are intended to guide learning and change at six key functional levels of the organization. They will help you use core strategies and core values as your "glue" and organizing principles. You will learn how to apply the concept of the levels of living systems so you can create rewards systems for all organizational levels and ensure the methods of communication in your company meet its systems needs.

TOOL NO.	THE APPLICATIONS
24.	"Glue" and the Cascade of Planning
25.	Six Leadership Competencies
26.	Total Rewards Systems—All Levels
27.	Methods of Communication
➡ These Tools Will Help You with Six Levels of Leadership and Management Functioning!	

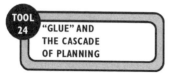

Application of
• Seven Levels of Living Systems
• Standard Systems Dynamics
  — 10. Interrelated Parts

Develop your strategic plan, operations plans, and project plans using the A-B-C-D systems phases and the different levels of living systems, including regular and annual strategic reviews and updates.

The Cascade of Planning

This planning method links all the levels of your organization, from corporate to business units to departments to teams to individuals (see Figure 20, on next page). Your core strategies (shorter-term desired results) and core values (guides to behavior) play a crucial role in the cascade of planning: they are your "glue" and organizing principles—what gives cohesive structure to your planning. Your basic steps here are thus the following:

1. Use your core strategies and core values as your glue and organizing principles.

2. Use the cascade of planning levels to link all organization levels to these strategies and values.

I suggest you use agreed-upon core strategies as your glue, so you can cascade planning to all major organizational departments. I also STRONGLY recommend you eliminate the concepts of business goals, department annual objectives, and individual key result areas (KRAs), replacing them with your overall core strategies. In this way, everybody and everywhere in the organization focuses on the same five or six integrated strategies you have rather than separate, solo, and functional "departments" and jobs.

FIGURE 20. THE CASCADE OF PLANNING

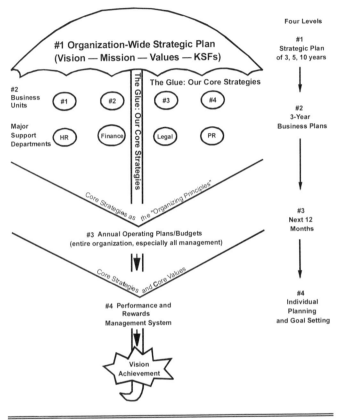

Priority of Strategies and Focus

With so many choices of outcomes and new technologies in today's rapidly changing environment, priority setting and focus at all levels is essential. You need to concentrate on a select few strategies, and on future priorities, not just the current situation.

➡ For Example

In personal planning as well as organization-wide strategic planning, it is crucial to focus on a small number of core strategies for success, even if that is difficult (and it usually is). You might have six core strategies for achieving your vision; less is better here.

Core Strategies and Priority of Annual Action Items

In any organization, you need to set priorities and focus for the top *three* actions under *each* core strategy for the next 12 months (this is another of example of the Rule of Threes). The question you must ask is, "In terms of ensuring overall success this year, what top priority action items must be accomplished?"

Use a format like the one below to chart the actions and their related concerns (add core strategies to the chart as needed). And remember, don't try to be all things to all people—it doesn't work.

SAMPLE CHART FORMAT: PRIORITY SETTING				
Core Strategies	Who Responsible?	Who to Involve?	When Done?	Status?
Core Strategy 1 (a) (b) (c)				
Core Strategy 2 (a) (b) (c)				

The Need for Focus

Once you have determined the action items, you must *focus, focus, focus* on achieving them. That focus needs to be operationalized—is a force behind the glue that holds organizations together. Remember that you implement *annual department plans,* not strategic plans.

➡ For Example

Organizations are typically organized vertically and downward, by specific factors and professions; however, work in organizations gets done horizontally, across functions.

Annual Departmental Plans

Cascading is easiest when all departmental plans are based on the same core strategies and work horizontally between functions, since all departments will have the same goals (or strategies as goals). Here is the procedure for such plans:

1. Each department builds its annual departmental plan using the same priority-setting charting format shown above.

2. The drafts of these plans are shared and critiqued in a large group meeting, with as many members of management there as possible and practical.

    Interestingly enough, the chart column that elicits the most comments is usually "Who to Involve?"—showing how little we know of our impact on others, that is, the relationship and fit of system components.

3. After this sharing of, and feedback on, department plans, the plans are finalized.

TASK

Department: _____

Date: _____
Fiscal Year: _____

Annual "Work Plan" Format
(and for Functional Division Work Plans also)

_____ : Strategy/Goals: _____

Yearly Pri#	Action Items (Actions/Objectives/How?)	Support/Resources Needed	Who Responsible?	Who Else to Involve?	When Done?	How to Measure? (Optional)	Status

Performance Appraisals

Performance appraisals are usually poorly accomplished tasks in most organizations. A *performance management system* is far preferable for each and every organization.

To tie your strategic plan to performance appraisal, you must link the key results areas (KRAs) of every job description to the organization's (1) core strategies and (2) core values. Do this by setting up the appraisal over three pages (in addition to a cover page):

- Page 1—Your organization's core strategies (results). Performance is appraised in relation to the core strategies.
- Page 2—Your organization's core values (behaviors). Performance is appraised in relation to adherence to the core values.
- Page 3—The individual's career development. Here career growth and development is considered, as well as the overall evaluation given.

GUIDELINES FOR USE

I.   Adopt this cascade of planning as part of your strategic management systems.

I.   Be aware that until you get the strategic plan down to your day-to-day decision making and annual performance appraisal, it is never fully successful.

2.   The need to prioritize action items applies to your personal life as well as professional one. Know your future vision and core strategies, and the means to achieve them. Then list your top three actions to accomplish each strategy.

TOOL 25 SIX LEADERSHIP COMPETENCIES

Application of
Seven Levels
of Living Systems

Before implementing a leadership development system, we need to know what competencies and skills a leader might need. If we apply the seven levels of living systems to this issue, we find there are six competencies areas (three systems levels and three collisions of systems levels) that are essential to leadership.

The "Centering Your Leadership" Model

Few people approach leadership development in systems terms (in researching 27 popular authors and more than 30 books on this topic, we[*] found that none looked at it in systems terms). Yet, once we apply systems thinking to leadership, we can see that the model offered in this tool only makes sense, pointing out precisely where leadership competencies are needed (see Figure 21, next page).

After developing this model, the Centre for Strategic Management looked at the many skills associated with the competencies. Using a Delphi technique, along with research, we reduced those skills to the five most crucial for each competency. The six competencies and their skills are as follows:

I. **Enhancing Self-Mastery**
  • Goal Setting
  • Integrating Development of My System
  • Acting With Conscious Intent
  • Ethics and Character Development
  • Accurate Self-Awareness

---

[*] "We" includes myself plus Chuck Gustafson, Jim Mckinlay, Salere Peekio, Dennis Rowley, and John Ash of the Centre for Strategic Management.

FIGURE 21. "CENTERING YOUR LEADERSHIP" MODEL

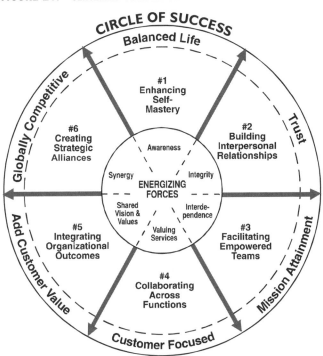

2. **Building Interpersonal Relationships**
   - Caring
   - Effectively Communicating
   - Mentoring and Coaching
   - Managing Conflict
   - Innovating and Creativity

3. **Facilitating Empowered Teams**
   - Practicing Participative Management
   - Facilitating Groups
   - Delegating and Empowering
   - Training
   - Building Effective Teams

4. **Collaborating Across Functions**
   - Installing Cross-Functional Teamwork
   - Integrating Business Processes
   - Valuing the Differences
   - Serving Others
   - Managing People Processes

5. **Integrating Organizational Outcomes**
   - Reinventing Strategic Planning
   - Mastering Strategic Communications
   - Positioning the Organization
   - Leading Cultural Change
   - Organizing and Designing

6. **Creating Strategic Alliances**
   - Scanning the Global Environment
   - Practicing Interest-Based Negotiations
   - Managing Alliances
   - Networking
   - International Effectiveness

Survey: Leadership Development Competencies

To tailor your personal leadership or your organization's leadership development trends, take the survey of 30 skills on the next two pages.

SURVEY: Leadership Development Competencies

SURVEY: LEADERSHIP DEVELOPMENT COMPETENCIES

Directions: Please rate yourself, or your organization, on the following skills areas.

CORE COMPETENCY Self: Organization:	CURRENT STATE ASSESSMENT										SCORE & COMMENTS
	(1) No Skills Reactive Org.				(5) Some Skills Responsible Org.					(10) High Skills High-Perf. Org.	
Level 1: Enhancing Self-Mastery											Level 1—Total Score:
1. Goal Setting	(1)	2	3	4	(5)	6	7	8	9	(10)	_____/5 =
2. Integrating Dev. of My System	(1)	2	3	4	(5)	6	7	8	9	(10)	_____ Average
3. Acting with Conscious Intent	(1)	2	3	4	(5)	6	7	8	9	(10)	
4. Ethics & Character Development	(1)	2	3	4	(5)	6	7	8	9	(10)	
5. Accurate Self-Awareness	(1)	2	3	4	(5)	6	7	8	9	(10)	
Level 2: Bldg. Interper. Relationships											Level 2—Total Score:
6. Caring	(1)	2	3	4	(5)	6	7	8	9	(10)	_____/5 =
7. Effectively Communicating	(1)	2	3	4	(5)	6	7	8	9	(10)	_____ Average
8. Mentoring & Coaching	(1)	2	3	4	(5)	6	7	8	9	(10)	
9. Managing Conflict	(1)	2	3	4	(5)	6	7	8	9	(10)	
10. Innovating & Creativity	(1)	2	3	4	(5)	6	7	8	9	(10)	
Level 3 : Facilitating Empwrd. Teams											Level 3—Total Score:
11. Practicing Participative Mgmt.	(1)	2	3	4	(5)	6	7	8	9	(10)	_____/5 =
12. Facilitating Groups	(1)	2	3	4	(5)	6	7	8	9	(10)	_____ Average
13. Delegating & Empowering	(1)	2	3	4	(5)	6	7	8	9	(10)	
14. Training	(1)	2	3	4	(5)	6	7	8	9	(10)	
15. Building Effective Teams	(1)	2	3	4	(5)	6	7	8	9	(10)	

SURVEY: LEADERSHIP DEVELOPMENT COMPETENCIES (*Concluded*)

CORE COMPETENCY	CURRENT STATE ASSESSMENT			SCORE & COMMENTS
Self: / Organization:	(1) No Skills / Reactive Org.	(5) Some Skills / Responsible Org.	(10) High Skills / High-Perf. Org.	
Level 4: Collaborating Across Functions				Level 4—Total Score: ___ /5 = ___ Average
16. Installing Cross-Funct. Teamwk.	(1) 2 3 4	(5)	6 7 8 9 (10)	
17. Integrating Business Processes	(1) 2 3 4	(5)	6 7 8 9 (10)	
18. Valuing the Differences	(1) 2 3 4	(5)	6 7 8 9 (10)	
19. Serving Others	(1) 2 3 4	(5)	6 7 8 9 (10)	
20. Managing People Processes	(1) 2 3 4	(5)	6 7 8 9 (10)	
Level 5: Integrating Org'l Outcomes				Level 5—Total Score: ___ /5 = ___ Average
21. Reinventing Strategic Planning	(1) 2 3 4	(5)	6 7 8 9 (10)	
22. Mastering Strat. Communications	(1) 2 3 4	(5)	6 7 8 9 (10)	
23. Positioning the Organization	(1) 2 3 4	(5)	6 7 8 9 (10)	
24. Leading Cultural Change	(1) 2 3 4	(5)	6 7 8 9 (10)	
25. Organizing & Designing	(1) 2 3 4	(5)	6 7 8 9 (10)	
Level 6: Creating Strategic Alliances				Level 6—Total Score: ___ /5 = ___ Average
26. Scanning the Global Environment	(1) 2 3 4	(5)	6 7 8 9 (10)	
27. Pract. Interest-Bsd. Negotiations	(1) 2 3 4	(5)	6 7 8 9 (10)	
28. Managing Alliances	(1) 2 3 4	(5)	6 7 8 9 (10)	
29. Networking	(1) 2 3 4	(5)	6 7 8 9 (10)	
30. International Effectiveness	(1) 2 3 4	(5)	6 7 8 9 (10)	
Grand Total ___ (300 possible)/30 = ___ Average				

GUIDELINES FOR USE

Use this tool to build development options for yourself
or your organization. These might include the following
"development" options.

Question: Which of these do we prefer to use for
development?

- ❏ Public seminars
- ❏ Executive seminars—universities
- ❏ Customized, in-house training
- ❏ Mentoring—shadowing—guide and confidante
- ❏ Professional associations
- ❏ Conference attendance
- ❏ Committees
- ❏ Practicums—action learning
- ❏ Intern programs
- ❏ Job rotation
- ❏ Temporary job assignment
- ❏ Job placement
- ❏ Task forces
- ❏ Vendor, field, headquarters visits
- ❏ Reading lists
- ❏ Buddy system support
- ❏ Train others
- ❏ Goal setting
- ❏ Body-Mind-Spirit assessment
- ❏ What else? _____

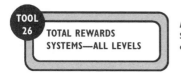

TOOL
26 TOTAL REWARDS
SYSTEMS—ALL LEVELS

Application of
Seven Levels
of Living Systems

One of the keys to organizational success is a total rewards system, both financial and non-financial, for (1) individuals, (2) teams, and (3) the entire organization. The rewards should be timely and meaningful to them, and should be linked to your strategic plan.

Survey Results: Employees' Needs

Nationwide survey results** indicate that employees' top three job needs are:

1. Recognition for doing good work
2. Freedom for independent thought and action
3. Opportunity for personal growth

Other needs include:

4. Higher salary and/or more benefits
5. Promotion to a better job
6. Job security
7. Satisfying the boss's wishes
8. Prestige and status

According to best-practices research (Haines, 1984, and updated), effective rewards are:

- Timely
- Significant
- Personally meaningful

---

* Source: Dr. H. Migliore, Dean, Oral Roberts Business School, and similar surveys conducted by the author across North America, Asia, and Europe.

- Gained through competing with only oneself
- Rewards with multiple winners

Note that "Pay for performance" violates all of these; hence, the need for a different type of reward—a non-financial one.

Innovative Non-Financial Rewards

Some innovative non-financial rewards that meet the top three job needs of employees include:

1. **Recognition**
   - Administrative Recognition Program (ICA)—after the fact
   - Thanks cards, letters, pictures, plaques, newsletters
   - Team celebration, dinners
   - Interteam, projects celebrations
   - Tokens—on-the-spot (Paul Revere Insurance)
   - "Academy Awards"
   - On-the-spot rewards
   - Seniority, service awards
   - Senior management visits
   - Company parties, meetings

2. **Freedom/Independent Thought and Actions**
   - IBM Presidents Club; Seoul Olympics (80/20 Rule)
   - Production team awards
   - ICA sales meetings, awards quarterly
   - Self-managed work teams
   - Flex-time, part-time
   - Task forces, project teams, quality
   - Empowerment, delegation

3. **Growth and Development**
   - Training attendance
   - Career development (IJP)
   - Job design (Plan—Do—Control)
   - Job rotation, pay for knowledge
   - Customer/Vendor trips
   - Professional development, associations

4. **Pay**
   - Fixed/Variable compensation (no merits)
   - Restricted stock, cliff vesting
   - Benefits: 401K, pension, time off
   - Corporate/Unit profit sharing
   - Deferred compensation: CD rates
   - ESOP
   - Immediate leader awards
   - Stock purchase plans

Employee Needs Questionnaire

What do employees want from a performance management system? To find out, have employees fill out the "needs" questionnaire on the following page. Organize the results; then use them to reexamine your current total rewards program. See if the results are the same as those I've observed over 100 times before and detailed at the beginning of this text.

GUIDELINES FOR USE

1. Use this tool's list of innovative rewards as a starting point to revamp your key non-financial rewards programs and processes.

2. Revamp your pay program, applying the best practices of effective rewards.

   Remember, those rewards must be (1) timely, (2) significant, (3) personally meaningful, (4) gained through "self-competition" only, and (5) ones where there are multiple winners.

3. See the exercise that closes this tool to diagnose your current total rewards program and determine what areas you need to change.

QUESTIONNAIRE: EMPLOYEE NEEDS

Directions: Below are listed 10 personal and job-related needs. Which ones matter the most to you? Please number these needs, listing them in priority rank order from 1 to 10, with 1 as your highest priority.

PRIORITY   **NEEDS**

☐   (a) Higher salary and more benefits

☐   (b) Recognition for doing good work

☐   (c) Food, clothing, and shelter

☐   (d) Satisfying the boss's wishes

☐   (e) Promotion to a better job

☐   (f) Personal growth and development

☐   (g) Safety in your work environment

☐   (h) Prestige and status

☐   (i) Job security

☐   (j) Opportunity for independent thought and action; freedom

Comments:

Diagnostic Exercise: Rewards for Total Performance

**Pay for
Position
and
Reward for
Performance**

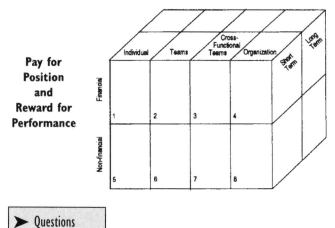

> **➤** Questions

1. Use the "rewards cube" above to diagnose how you are currently rewarding your (1) people, (2) teams, and (3) organization as a whole.

2. Use it to look at both your current short-term and long-term rewards.

3. Use it to look at both financial and non-financial rewards.

4. Compare your answers to questions 1, 2, and 3 above vs. the innovative rewards list given earlier in this tool. The big question is whether or not you are providing the top three rewards people want, as shown earlier in this tool.

5. Lastly, what areas do you need to change?

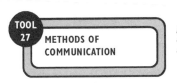

TOOL 27 METHODS OF COMMUNICATION

Application of
• Seven Levels of Living Systems
• Standard Systems Dynamics
  — 5. Feedback

In today's dynamic and fast-paced environment, we are hard-pressed to communicate as frequently and effectively as we would prefer. To compensate for this, we have developed new, high-tech communications methods such as E-mail, answering machines, faxes, and the like. However, they are all "one-way" methods, and good communication requires *two active partners,* the sender and the receiver, and the chance for immediate response and exchange of any further information needed.

The Ineffectiveness of One-Way Communication

Too much of our quick communication today is one-way, with the sheer volume of E-mail, letters, faxes, and other one-way messages taxing our ability to *really* hear and understand others. Moreover, we often rely on visual and auditory cues, such as body language and vocal inflection, to fully grasp what others are trying to communicate to us, and to gauge how *our* message is being understood by others. One-way communication, which gives us neither cues nor feedback, is thus relatively ineffective by itself.

➡ For Example

While E-mail can be quick and fast, it is a one-way method and impersonal in nature. Because the lack of cues and feedback can lead to misconstrued meanings, such communication is far more apt to result in angry, conflict-generating messages than two-way, face-to-face communication.

FIGURE 22. LADDER OF COMMUNICATION EFFECTIVENESS

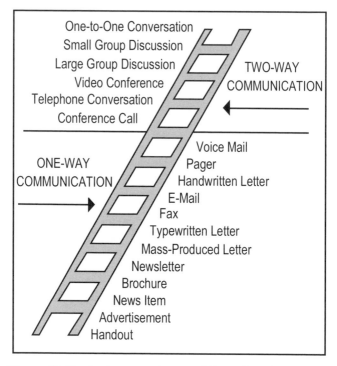

Figure 22, illustrates our point, providing a list of communication methods from the most effective to the least.

Repetition—Repetition—Repetition

People do not hear, and certainly do not understand, everything you say to them. Or they simply may not believe it. What can you do about this problem? You can *repeat* what you have to say, perhaps even three or four times, to get your message across and to ensure your message is *remembered*.

Repetition and "stump speeches" are crucial for helping
people through change, especially when the situation is
an emotional one. As the following statistics show, people
need to hear such messages a number of times to feel most
comfortable with, and to understand, what you have to say.

Communication Methods	
Words	= 7%
Vocal Tone	= 38%
Body Language	= 55%
Total	= 100%

**What you do speaks louder
than what you say!**

We Recall Approximately

- 10% of what we *read*
- 20% of what we *hear*
- 30% of what we *see*
- 50% of what we *see & hear*
- 70% of what we *say & do*
- 90% of what we *explain as
  we do*

**Repetition Increases
Understanding**

- 1st time = 10% retention
- 2nd time = 25% retention
- 3rd time = 40%–50% retention
- 4th time = 75% retention

Strategic Communications Matrix

Set up a strategic communications matrix and/or a
"proposed rollout plan" matrix (see sample on the next
page) for communicating change strategically to all your
stakeholders. Use the systems concept of the seven levels of
living systems as a guide for creating your communications
matrix.

SAMPLE MATRIX: PROPOSED ROLLOUT PLAN (OF ANY CHANGE)						
Key Stakeholders	Method of Rollout	Who Responsible?	Resources Needed?	Who Else to Involve?	Key Issues to Address	Status of Completion?
1. Employees						
2. Middle Mgmt.						
3. Customers						
4. Vendors						
5. Share-holders						
6. Community						
7. Others						

Matrices as Systems Tools

Matrices are great to show relationships between systems or systems concepts. Simply set up a matrix of the components or systems you want to analyze. Then work down the vertical column, comparing each component to those in the top row; fill in the matrix with your comments, and draw the needed conclusions. This is a good way to build action plans.

GUIDELINES FOR USE

1. Analyze your communication methods, or better yet, get a trusted friend or colleague to help you. Focus on these questions:

   • Which methods to you use most of time?

   • Which two-way communications do you underuse?

   • Which one-way communications do you overuse?

   • What changes must you make to be a more effective communicator?

2. When communicating, use body language, vocal tone, and other visual/auditory signals to better convey your meaning.

3. Teach what you want to learn yourself. You will be more focused on the material and more aware of communicating the material clearly and comprehensively. Your enthusiasm will facilitate communication!

VII. The Rollercoaster of Change

The application in this chapter focuses on the concept most essential to guiding organizational change: that of changing systems, the natural cycles of life and change. As we saw in Chapter I, this concept can be expressed as the *Rollercoaster of Change.* We will look at the Rollercoaster's many uses, particularly its application for self-, interpersonal, team, and organizational change.

TOOL NO.	THE APPLICATIONS
28.	**Managing the Rollercoaster of Change** —*The Rollercoaster of Self-Change* —*The Rollercoaster of Interpersonal Change* —*The Rollercoaster of Team Change* —*The Rollercoaster of Organizational Change*
	➡ **These Tools Will Help You Guide Organizational Change!**

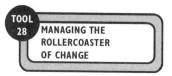

Application of
• Seven Levels of Living Systems
• Changing Systems: The Natural
  Cycles of Life and Change

A. THE ROLLERCOASTER OF CHANGE & SYSTEMS THINKING

Systems work in natural cycles and circular ways, which is quite a departure from our more familiar, analytic and linear way of thinking about the world. We must keep in mind that the Rollercoaster of Change is a natural and normal part of life. Change cycles and input-throughput-output-feedback cycles occur endlessly throughout the seven levels of living systems as systems levels interact with one another. And we are a part of such systems.

➤ **For Example**

When we go through change, whether personal or professional, we don't move on a straight line of productivity from *a* to *b*. Our thoughts, feelings, and experiences fluctuate between highs and lows; we feel as if we are on a rollercoaster.

Often, just knowing about the Rollercoaster of Change helps people who are undergoing change. They see it is only natural to experience difficulties at such times. The key is "hanging in there," in developing persistence.

Nothing in the world can take the place of persistence. Talent will not; nothing is more common than unsuccessful men with talent. Genius will not; unrewarded genius is almost a proverb. Education will not; the world is full of educated derelicts. Persistence and determination alone are omnipotent.

—Calvin Coolidge

A basic truth of management—if not of life—is that nearly everything looks like a failure in the middle . . . persistent, consistent execution is unglamorous, time-consuming, and sometimes boring.

—Rosabeth Moss Kanter, 1990

Change: An Experience of Loss

We can manage the Rollercoaster of Change better if we understand that people experiencing change typically feel a deep sense of loss. They are heading toward new territory, with old, familiar ways—always so comfortable, and often valued—falling behind them. Harry Levinson's insights in *Psychological Man* give us a foundation for understanding loss and its effects on people and organizational change. The following helpful points are based on his work.

1. Loss creates a feeling of depression for most people. One loses preferred modes of attaining and giving affection, handling aggression, dependency needs— all those *familiar routines* which we have evolved and usually taken for granted.
2. Loss is a difficult experience to handle, particularly if what one leaves behind is psychologically important.
3. All loss must be mourned and the attendant feelings disgorged if a restitution process is to operate effectively.
4. Most organization change flounders because the experience of loss is not taken into account. *To undertake successful organizational change, an executive must anticipate and provide the means of working through that loss and all four phases of it.*

The four phases of working through loss are clearly shown in basic model for the Rollercoaster of Change, on the next page.

FIGURE 23. MODEL: CHANGE AND SYSTEMS THINKING

The Rollercoaster of Change and Systems Thinking

Perseverance — The Key to Strategic Change

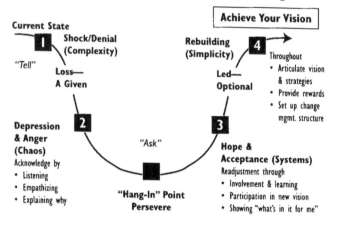

Chaos and Complexity

Chaos and complexity are a normal and natural part of the process of change—of discovering new ways of being and achieving new visions

The Major Change-Related Questions

When planning to undertake any change effort, you need to ask, and answer, 12 important change-related questions. They will prepare you and others for the "rollercoaster" to come, and help you acknowledge the difficulties of change.

The 12 Change-Related Questions

1. Not if, but when will we start to go through shock and depression?

2. How deep is the trough? Is it different for each person? (What are the implications?)

3. How long will it take? Are employees and management at the same stage?

4. Will we get up the right (optional) side and rebuild?

5. How do we manage the change proactively?

6. At what level will we rebuild?

7. What new skills do we need to accomplish this?

8. How many different rollercoasters will we experience during this change?

9. Are there other changes (with their own rollercoasters) occurring?

10. Will we hang in and persevere at the midpoint (the lowest point)? How?

11. How will we deal with normal resistance? (Push or pull?)

12. How will we create a critical mass to support and achieve the change?

The Many Uses of the Rollercoaster of Change

This model is what you need to know to predict, lead, and manage any type of change, personal or professional.

➡ For Example

Learning, training, planning, team building, and the like are just different types of change; our model can help manage all of them.

Variations of the basic model are provided later in this tool, illustrating its use for self-, interpersonal, team, and organizational change.

Important Points to Remember

Whatever you are doing personally and professionally in today's world, it likely involves some form of change. You may not call it that, but that's what it is. So becoming an expert on the natural, predictable cycle of change is essential. To get there, keep in mind:

- Planning is really *planning for change.*

- Organizations change when people change, so change is actually a personal issue, involving behavioral change for each of us.

- We can't really change others. If we want others to change, we need to model that change in our own behavior and our relationships with others; usually only then is there a possibility of others changing.

GUIDELINES FOR USE

1. Internalize the Rollercoaster of Change and its sequences. Of course, be sure to remember that any model is only a simple representation of a complex reality.

2. Share this model with key people whenever you are involved in any type of change. Ensure people know it is natural and expected for things to get worse (Stage 2: Anger/Depression) before they get better (Stage 3 and 4) when change is involved.

3. Once you know the fundamentals, look at the other models in this tool and apply their terminology and actions to your specific situation.

B. THE ROLLERCOASTER OF SELF-CHANGE

Self-change is the first key level within the seven levels of living systems—for us personally, professionally, and organizationally. Our self-change model is shown below.

FIGURE 24. MODEL: SELF-CHANGE

The Rollercoaster of Self-Change

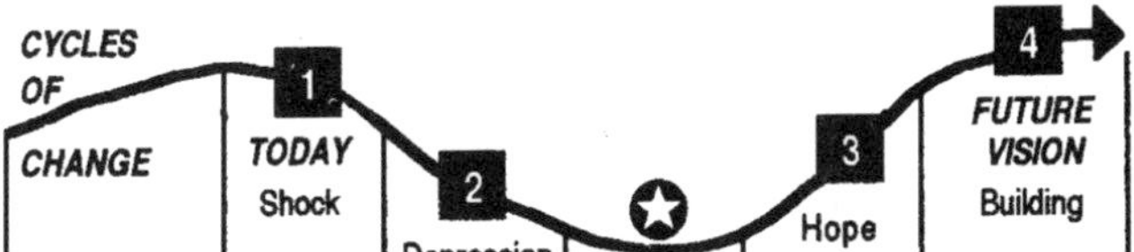 CYCLES OF CHANGE / USES	TODAY Shock (1)	Depression (2)	"Hang-In" (★)	Hope (3)	FUTURE VISION Building (4)
Self-Change 1. Understanding People/Change	Shock & Denial	Depression/ Anger/ Blame	Maximum Immobili- zation	Hope/ Acknowl./ Readjust (Accept.)	Rebldg./ Constructive Work
2. Employee Actions	Don't Overreact	Ask Questions/ Express Feelings/ Be Skeptical	Don't Give Up	Get Involved/ Answer WIITM/ Be Hopeful	Understand Vision/Be Committed/ Take Action/ Fit Into System

GUIDELINES FOR USE

I. **Learn this model well. Realize the curve of change is normal and natural; you're always somewhere on the curve, but wherever it is, you are, and will be, okay. Also realize that to help others with change, you yourself must get to Stage 3 (Hope) at a minimum.**

(Continued)

179

GUIDELINES FOR USE
(Concluded)

2. Don't deny your feelings and emotions when you are at Stage 2; acknowledge them. Take care of yourself; adopt coping behaviors—take time off, eat healthy, get enough sleep and exercise.

3. As an employee, follow the advice for each stage of the curve; especially, "Don't overreact."

C. THE ROLLERCOASTER OF INTERPERSONAL CHANGE

Interpersonal skills are obviously essential to success in your personal and professional life. Since change is constant for you and everyone else you come in contact with daily, it is important that you be able to handle the five interpersonal situations shown Figure 25, the Rollercoaster of Interpersonal Change.

➡ **For Example**

Inclusion, control, growth, openness, and performance are issues for all of us as we interact with others every day. They are natural and normal—go on all the time.

GUIDELINES FOR USE

1. Study the five situations presented in the model, and decide for yourself how you can become flexible enough in your own style to deal effectively with them.

2. Examine your level of openness. Do you initiate self-disclosure, or do you "guard your cards"? Are you willing to be open to feedback even if it hurts, so you can continue to learn, grow, and be more effective?

(Continued)

FIGURE 25. MODEL: INTERPERSONAL CHANGE

The Rollercoaster of Interpersonal Change

CYCLES OF CHANGE / USES	**1** TODAY Shock	**2** Depression	★ "Hang-In"	**3** Hope	**4** FUTURE VISION Building
Interpers. Chge. 1. Relationships	Inclusion Desire	Control Issues	Growth Desire	Openness	High Performance
2. Structure of Management Interactions w/Employees	Highly Directive/ Low Supportive	Highly Directive/ Highly Supportive	Transition/ Persistance	Highly Supportive/ Low Directive	Low Supportive/ Low Directive
3. Situation Leadership* (New Leadership Skills)	Tell/ Direct (Train)	Sell/Ask (Coach)	Persevere	Participate Involvement (Facilitate)	Delegate Within System (Empower)
4. Management's Specific Tasks	Change Self First/ Appreciate ("Everyone changes at different rates.")	Empathize/ Listen/ Explain Why/ Face-to-Face Mtgs./ Appreciate Skeptics	Be Consistent/ Model the Way	Seek Involvement/Show WIIFM/ Challenge Process/ Celebrate	Shared Vision/ Articulate Again & Again/ Enable Others/ Systems Fit, Alignment
5. Coaching	Contact/ Purpose	Chaos or Complexity	Continuous Relationship	Contract/ Norms	Collaboration/ Work

*SOURCE: Paul Hersey and Kenneth Blanchard

GUIDELINES FOR USE
(Concluded)

3. Be clear on how to interact with others on your own needs and theirs for inclusion and control. Realize that control needs often stifle growth.

4. Learn to be flexible. Try to match up your management style with the needs of others and their situation (hence the long-term popularity of Hersey & Blanchard's situation leadership model, on which the third situation in our model is based).

5. Acquire skills in active listening and questioning as well as in conveying knowledge and answering questions. Most of us tend to be good at only one side of this equation in our interpersonal relationships.

6. Use the model as a guide for improving your skills in coaching others. Learn effective listening skills; maintain the relationship between you and the person you are coaching, even when strong correction is necessary; build healthy norms between you both, including a clear sense of purpose and outcomes.

D. THE ROLLERCOASTER OF TEAM CHANGE

The success of organizations, families, and communities depends on groups of people working together productively as teams. Whenever people form new teams or join existing ones, it is natural for them to go through the team version of the Rollercoaster of Change, as shown in Figure 26.

➡ **For Example**

Most people assume that by putting groups of people together into a meeting, they have formed an effective team—one that can immediately do productive work. But nothing could be further from the truth.

FIGURE 26. MODEL: TEAM CHANGE

The Rollercoaster of Team Change

CYCLES OF CHANGE / USES	1 TODAY Shock	2 Depression	★ "Hang-In"	3 Hope	4 FUTURE VISION Building
Team Change 1. Group Dynamics Stages	Forming	Storming	Hang-In Point	Norming	Performing
2. Dialogue & Discovery	Denial	Defend	Discussion	Dialogue (Two-way= Learning	Discovery (of Applications)
3. Learning Stages (People/Teams/ Organizations)	Activity/ Experience	"What?" Process the Activity/ Feelings/ Trends	Transition to Learning/ Action	"So What?" So What Have We Learned? (Learnings)	"Now What?" Apply the Learnings (Application)
4. Conflict	Conflict	Raw Debate/ Polite Talk	Desire for Resolution	Disciplines Dialogue (Skills)	Skillful Discovery (Seek Truth)

GUIDELINES FOR USE

I. Most productive work requires teams to function effectively; therefore it is important to internalize the four stages of team/group dynamics:

1. Forming	3. Norming
2. Storming	4. Performing

(Continued)

GUIDELINES FOR USE *(Concluded)*

2. Learn techniques for speeding up this rollercoaster or learning curve of effective teamwork. Spend time at the beginning of teamwork to define the following:
   - Your purpose(s)
   - Your norms of acceptable behavior
   - Goals and timetables
   - Roles and accountabilities and their interdependencies
   - A feedback method to continually improve the team

3. Work with each team you are a member of to learn how to maintain intellectual honesty and the dialogue and discovery of better solutions that come with it—that is, learn to "leave your shield at the door" and stop defending your ideas and taking issues personally. You can either defend your position/ideas, or expand your range of information for better decision making; you cannot do both.

4. *Consensus* in decision making means that you can *actively support* the decision that is made. Work towards making this an effective tool in your teams.

5. Effective conflict resolution also goes through the stages of change. Stifling anger and emotions in the name of politeness and logic is to suppress conflict and its potential benefits. What are its benefits?

6. "Adults learn best by doing" is a basic truism. To learn from anything you are doing, whether a formal training program, a meeting, or the like, you must gain feedback and insights for improvement at the end of each activity. Do so by asking these three questions:
   1. *What* just happened?
   2. *So what* can we learn or generalize from all of this?
   3. *Now what* can we do to improve matters by applying these learnings?

E. THE ROLLERCOASTER OF ORGANIZATIONAL CHANGE

While organizations change when people change, there still is a collective set of behavioral changes the total organization must undergo to deal with constant and dynamic environmental change. This, then, is the ultimate level of living systems for improved organization effectiveness. And just as with (and within) the hierarchy of the seven levels of living systems, organizational change includes the rollercoaster dynamics of "lower" systems levels: the self, the interpersonal, and the team (see other change models, this chapter). Moreover, organization life cycles, strategies, and culture usually need to change as well.

➡ For Example

> Most organizations attempt organization-wide change in a piecemeal, haphazard fashion. This is why estimates are that 70 percent to 90 percent of all major change efforts fail.

In closely examining the Rollercoaster of Organizational Change (Figure 27, next page), keep in mind that major change requires close attention to, and fit between and among, all aspects of the web of relationships (parts or components) in support of the overall objectives of the whole system (organization). This includes:

- Individual, interpersonal, team/department cross-functions and organization-wide changes
- Alignment of your delivery processes based on the strategies you need in order to achieve world-class "star results" and customer value (Phase A, Outcomes; see number 2 in our model).
- Attunement of people's hearts and minds in support of the new values and desired culture (see number 4 in our model).

FIGURE 27. MODEL: ORGANIZATIONAL CHANGE

The Rollercoaster of Organizational Change

CYCLES OF CHANGE USES	TODAY 1 Shock	Depression 2	★ "Hang-In"	Hope 3	FUTURE VISION 4 Building
Org'l Change 1. Strategic Mgmt. System (includes Strategic Change)	Where Are We Today? (Current-State Assess.)	What Actions Do We Need to Take? (Content, Processes, & Structures)			Where Do We Want to Be? (Our Vision, Values, & Measures)
		"Holding On"	"Letting Go"	Alignment/ Fit of Parts	
2. Two Different Strategies (Alignment)	I. "Cutting" Staff Cuts/Reorganize/ Cost-Focused		Fit of Systems Persevere; Don't Back Off	II. "Building" Future Vision/Strategies/ Quality/Service/ "Customer-Focused"	
3. Org'l Life Cycle	Maturity	Decline	Death or Renewal	Growth	New Maturity
4. Cultural/Values Change (Attunement)	Shock/ Unfreeze Status Quo	Control/ Education, Communica- tions, Rewards/ Sanctions	Rebuild Morale/ Motivation	Create Critical Mass	Reward/ Empower New Culture

➡ Remember to Align Your Delivery Processes,
Attune People's Hearts and Minds,
and Develop a Strategic Management System

- A strategic management system that includes building a process for strategic change management. (The basic model of the Rollercoaster of Change is useful in this regard; also, we will look at strategic management in the next chapter.)

As the above list suggests, achieving major large-scale or transformational change is enormously difficult, with a low probability of success. However, by using the systems approach, you will increase the likelihood of success.

The Four Choices of Change

When it comes to organizational change, you have four options, as shown in Figure 28. Which option will you choose? What price are you willing to pay to achieve it?

FIGURE 28. THE FOUR CHOICES OF CHANGE

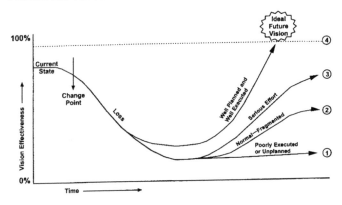

The Difficulties of Transformational Change

In dealing with change, be prepared to manage these difficult issues:

- Everyone changes at different rates and depths.

- Management undergoes change before rank-and-file employees.

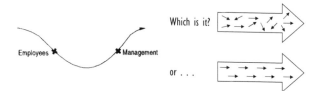

- All parts of the organization must fit and work together for the overall objective of the whole.

  For example:

  — Marketing
  — Manufacturing
  — HR Practices
  — MIS/Technology
  — Legal
  — Operations
  — Public Relations
  — Employee Involvement
  — Mission
  — Strategy
  — Values/Culture

  — Leadership/Management Staffing
  — Finance/Budgets
  — Communications
  — Organization Design
  — Personnel/Payroll
  — Business Processes
  — Tasks/Goals
  — Teamwork Rewards/Feedback
  — R & D
  — Engineering

- The sense of loss may be overwhelming, making it that much more difficult to manage the change situation.

Handling the Sense of Loss

Employees' sense of loss is a highly important issue, requiring direct and extensive work on Stage 2, Depression and Anger. The following checklist will help you focus on your major concerns in this area.

CHECKLIST: STAGE 2 CONCERNS & STRATEGIES

Directions: Check off your concerns regarding Stage 2 of the Rollercoaster of Change; then develop strategies to deal with them.

❑	1.	Loss of Influence
❑	2.	Loss of Control
❑	3.	Loss of Money
❑	4.	Concerns About Family Reaction to Change
❑	5.	Loss of Social Status
❑	6.	Concerns About Starting Over—Being the "New Kid"
❑	7.	Loss of Future
❑	8.	Loss of Relationships, Networks
❑	9.	Loss of Autonomy
❑	10.	Loss of Professional Identity
❑	11.	Loss of Territory
❑	12.	Concerns About Ability to Handle New Group
❑	13.	Loss of Role

(Continued)

CHECKLIST: STAGE 2 CONCERNS & STRATEGIES *(Concluded)*

- ❏ 14. Loss of Employment
- ❏ 15. Loss of Meaning
- ❏ 16. Concerns About Competency
- ❏ 17. Fear of Failure
- ❏ 18. Loss of Satisfaction
- ❏ 19. Loss of Support

STRATEGIES

APPLICATIONS

VIII. Summary Tool:
A Strategic Management System

The application in this chapter will help you set the previous tools in this guidebook into the context of a strategic management system. Its guiding systems concept is holism, which emphasizes the whole is not just the sum of its parts—that the system itself can only be explained as a totality. Holism requires total, strategic organizational management, with the integration of systems tools an essential part of that management. It is one of the most fundamental necessities of success in today's organizations.

TOOL NO.	THE APPLICATIONS
29.	**Strategic Management System** —*Including the 15 key benefits of a strategic management system, and a diagnostic tool for managing problems in your organization*

➡ **These Tools Will Help You Diagnose Organizational Problems and also Build a System of Managing Your Team, Department, or Organization in a More Strategic and Systems Fashion!**

TOOL 29 STRATEGIC MANAGEMENT SYSTEM

Application of
Standard Systems Dynamics
— I. Holism

Success in today's world requires a systems approach to managing your organization in a more complete, strategic fashion. The tools you have learned in this guidebook will help you, but you must use them in an integrated fashion. A strategic management system is thus a fundamental necessity.

The quotations below are highly useful for illuminating our topic here.

Organizations as Systems

Every organization is perfectly designed to get the results it is getting. Thus, if results are less than desired, the design should be changed. That includes adjusting structure, work processes, linkages, information flows, and functions to meet new needs.

—Quetico Centre,
Keeping Current (Fall 1994)

The Need for a Basic Reorientation of Our Thinking

In one way or another, we are forced to deal with complexities, with "wholes" or "systems" in all fields of knowledge. This implies a basic reorientation in scientific thinking.

—Ludwig Van Bertalanffy

The Need a Strategic Management System

I need to stress at this point that an effective management system is more than just the sum of the parts . . . it is a set of integrated policies, practices, and behaviors.

Sometimes having a good management system is confused with having high-quality employees. This is a mistake—the two are quite different. . . . Having high-quality employees does not assure an organization of having a sustainable competitive advantage or even a short-term advantage.

—Edward J. Lawler III,
*The Ultimate Advantage: Creating
the High-Involvement Organization* (1992)

The Winning Formula

Preparation, discipline, and talent, working within the system, is the winning playoff formula.

—Michael D. Mitchell, St. Louis
Sporting News, (May 16, 1994)

> **Strategic Management System:**
> *The Imperative for Survival!*

The Definition of a Strategic Management System

A strategic management system can be defined as:

- A comprehensive system to lead, manage, and change our total organization in a conscious, well planned out, and integrated fashion, based on our core strategies (and using *research that works*) to develop and achieve our ideal future vision.

- A *new* way to run the business; to manage business in a systematic way based on our strategies.

- An interactive and participative method in which people help create the system. *And people support what they help create*—this is a basic truth.

193

- A method managed as a complete systems change (with strategic/annual/individual plans, budgets, and measurements)

- A successful method if it is . . .
  1. Inspired by a common vision and shared
  2. Mission-focused/customer-focused
  3. Based on organizational values and culture
  4. Strategically driven
  5. Oriented towards outcomes and results

A strategic management system's hallmark is *strategic consistency yet operational flexibility (focus, focus, focus).*

The 15 Key Benefits of a Strategic Management System

Look closely at these 15 benefits. Are some of them missing from your organization?

1. Taking an organization-wide, proactive approach to a changing global world

2. Building an executive team that serves as a model of cross-functional or horizontal teamwork

3. Having an intense executive development and strategic orientation process

4. Defining focused, quantifiable outcome measures of success

5. Making intelligent budgeting decisions

6. Clarifying your competitive advantage

7. Reducing conflict; empowering the organization

8. Providing clear guidelines for day-to-day decision making

9. Creating a critical mass for change

10. "Singing from the same hymnal" throughout the organization

11. Clarifying and simplifying the barrage of management techniques

12. Empowering middle managers

13. Focusing everyone in the organization on the same overall framework

14. Speeding up implementation of the core strategies

15. Providing tangible tools for handling the stress of change

Diagnostic Checklist: Strategic Management System

The checklist below will help you examine your organization to spot any dysfunctional areas that still require problem solving and action.

DIAGNOSTIC CHECKLIST: STRATEGIC MANAGEMENT SYSTEM		
Directions: Which of these problems do you face? Rate each problem's severity from high (H) to medium (M) to low (L); then decide what actions are needed.		
H - M - L	**OUTPUT (PROBLEM)**	**WHAT IS PROBABLY MISSING**
☐ ☐ ☐	1. Conflict and survival	**Ideal Future Vision** (Not shared; plus others below)
☐ ☐ ☐	2. Success unknown (except financial)	**Measurement System** (Not in place/accountability)
☐ ☐ ☐	3. Confusion and all things to all people	**Core Strategies** (No consensus; no list of top-priority items)
☐ ☐ ☐	4. Low implementation of quality/service	**Operational Tasks** (No dept. annual plans or accountability/follow-up)
☐ ☐ ☐	5. Incompetence and blaming	**Leadership and Management Skills** (No values on appraisal)
☐ ☐ ☐	6. Low commitment and incrementalism	**Resources** (Unfocused; no priorities)

(Continued)

DIAGNOSTIC CHECKLIST: STRATEGIC MANAGEMENT SYSTEM *(Concluded)*		
H-M-L	**OUTPUT (PROBLEM)**	**WHAT IS PROBABLY MISSING**
☐ ☐ ☐	7. Bureaucracy and fragmentation	Organizational Design (Unknown or traditional)
☐ ☐ ☐	8. Low risk-taking, poor people management	HR and Rewards System (Missing; not tied to values/strategies)
☐ ☐ ☐	9. Adversarial environment	Interdepartment Teamwork (Not focused upon/rewarded)
☐ ☐ ☐	10. No follow-through	Strategic Change Management System (Missing system and accountability)

PROBLEM	ACTION NEEDED?

Using an Annual Strategic Review

It should be obvious by now that this book's tools are only part of an overall system of *how to lead and manage an organization in a systematic and strategic fashion*. Good organizations have this system, and they review it formally every year as part of an annual strategic review and update of the organization's overall direction (see Figure 29, below).

FIGURE 29. YEARLY STRATEGIC MANAGEMENT CYCLE

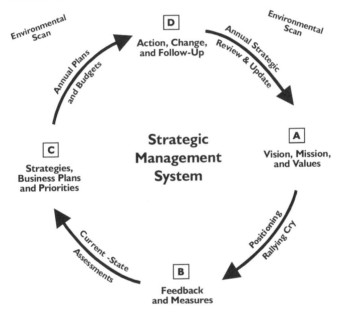

This review focuses equally on all the components of the A-B-C-D framework, namely, the customer (Phase A), feedback and learning (Phase B), the entire strategic plan (Phase C), and action, change, and follow-up (Phase D). It includes the need for a strategic change management process governing and guiding the alignment of delivery processes and the attunement of people's hearts and minds.

The annual strategic review is the way to refresh, update, and renew your vision and direction as well as your implementation plans. Only by doing this once a year in a formal fashion (along with weekly, monthly, and quarterly follow-up processes) will you be assured you have designed and built—and are sustaining—a strategic management system that is taking you in a long-term positive direction. This is what assists you year after year in achieving your ideal future vision (for a detailed look at this, see *Sustaining High Performance,* Haines, 1994).

What is *your* ideal future vision? It should linked to seeing your customer as *the* most important outcome of any organization as a system—or of any person living a fulfilling life. Draw on the tools you have learned in this guidebook: they will help you create customer value in both your personal life and your organizational career, so you can make that ideal future vision a reality.

CONCLUSION

IX. Summary of
Systems Thinking and Learning

Systems thinking offers us a better way of expressing ourselves, understanding the world, and living our personal and professional lives than do the old analytic and mechanistic thinking modes. The systems perspective gives us a better view on our "radar scope" and thus a more effective method of thought, communication, problem solving, and action. Without it, today's thinking and problem solving become the source of tomorrow's problems.

THE NEW LANGUAGE OF SYSTEMS

People and organizations need to do more than just use systems tools; they need to adopt systems terminology and systems-oriented questions into their everyday vocabulary. These help clarify and simplify "solution seeking," bringing into solutions a more holistic light.

To get you started, here is a review of some of the key terms, principles, and questions of systems thinking.

1. *A-B-C-D model or framework.* Specifically:

    A. Output   C. Input
    B. Feedback   D Throughput

    —Within E. The Environment

By using this framework, we simplify and better manage the chaos and confusion that confronts us. We have more of a chance to see the forest *and* the trees.

2. *Question: What entity (system or "collision of systems") are we dealing with?* This is the preliminary systems question.

3. Basic phase-associated questions:
   A. *Where do we want to be?*
   B. *How will we know we have reached it?*
   C. *Where are we now?*
   D. *How do we get from here to our desired place?*
   And E. The ongoing question throughout all phases:
   What is changing in the environment that we need to consider?

4. *Means and ends*

5. *Multiple goal seeking*

6. *Strategic consistency and operational flexibility*

7. *"Backwards thinking."* Begin with the end in mind.

8. Principle: *The whole is primary, the parts secondary.*

9. *Synthesis* as a new way of thinking, as opposed to the analytic thinking.

10. Principle: *In the environment, living systems interact in a hierarchy.*

11. Feedback stimulates learning and change; it is "the breakfast of champions."

12. *Negative entropy or positive energy.* This is continuously needed in a system; feedback is essential for managing it.

13. *Relationships and fit are key.* Processes are important—are not separate events.

14. *Multiple causes and effects*
    - Causes and effects are circular, not linear.
    - They are not necessarily related in a direct, immediate way.

15. Simplistic, quick fixes do not work!

16. Systems concept: Seven levels of living systems. In this book, we have been primarily concerned with four levels:
    3. Individual
    4. Group/Team
    5. Organization
    6. Society/Community

17. KISS method—reduces complexity, rigidity, bureaucracy, and total systems failure.

18. General Systems Theory—Work closely with the material in this guidebook until you have a firm understanding of these terms, principles, and questions, and can use them comfortably.

THE BENEFITS OF SYSTEMS THINKING AND LEARNING

Systems thinking has a number of far-reaching benefits, providing us with:

1. An overall framework for making sense out of life's complexities and its many systems. This framework allows us to detect patterns and relationships between systems, and between systems and their levels, leading to better problem solving.

2. A way to learn new things more easily. Its basic rules are simple and consistent—they stay the same from system to system.

3. A better approach for integrating new ideas within the systems context.

4. A clearer way to see and understand what is going on in any organization or any system and its environment. Complex problems become easier to understand, as do the interrelationships of parts and multiple cause-and-effect cycles.

5. A new and better way to create strategies, problem-solve, and find leverage points—keeping the outcome/vision/goal in mind at all times.

6. The key questions of systems thinking and an A-B-C-D template with which to correctly begin any diagnostic or discovery work—problem solving and solution seeking.

7. A way to engage teams and people in a deeper thought process, analysis, and definition of root causes, thus leading to longer-lasting results. It enables groups to generate multiple choices and different solutions, rather than just quick-fix answers, when working with difficult problems.

8. A method for getting at the deeper structure and relationship of process issues—things that are missed by the "quick-fix" mentality.

9. A challenge to the inaccurate assumptions and mental models that guide our thinking, acting, and problem solving. When such factors hold us back, it usually means new, broader, longer-lasting solutions do not get identified and implemented and that creative possibilities are overlooked.

10. A view of the dynamic interactions and relationships of a system's elements and the collision of the system with other systems; we thus make better decisions, with a clearer understanding of the consequences.

11. A better framework for diagramming, mapping, diagnosing, and analyzing any system—department, unit, organization, or otherwise. It improves our problem solving and decision making for that system.

12. A way to manage the complex Systems Age by focusing on the whole, its components, and the interrelationships of the components, rather than by focusing on supposedly isolated and independent parts and problems.

13. A common framework and model for thinking and communicating, so people can work together better to make positive change in any system and achieve the desired outcomes.

THE KEYS TO SUCCESS IN THE SYSTEMS AGE

What keys do we need to successfully let go of old ways and grab hold of newer, more effective ways? They lie in us becoming "paradigm pioneers," to borrow a term from Joel Barker. To fully embrace the Systems Age, and to fully integrate our systems tools, each of us must be willing to do the following:

- Go beyond our own borders and rules

- Break the rules of past success, *not wait until they're broken*

- Develop new reading habits: *suspend our judgment*

- Be ready for failure, not avoid it: *from failure springs the seeds of future success*

- Actively listen to other, rather than prepare our response to them; therefore listen, listen, *listen!*

When all is said and done, we will successfully integrate systems solutions to our systems problems only when we make the transition from unconscious to conscious systems applications, terminology, and language.

Organizations *need* systems thinking and its integrative approach to problem solving. Thinking across boundaries, or integrative systems thinking, is the ultimate entrepreneurial act. Call it business creativity. Call it holistic thinking. To see problems and opportunities integratively is to see them as wholes related to larger wholes, rather than as discrete bits assigned to distinct, separate categories that never influence or touch one another. Research has associated this way of thinking with higher levels of organizational innovation, personal creativity, and even longer life. Clearly we, as individuals, need systems thinking too.

> **How You Think . . . Is How You Act . . .**
> **Is How Your Are!**

When we look at resolving today's problems in order to grow and thrive in a brand-new age, we must always remind ourselves that *how we approach issues* and *how we think about them* are just as crucial as *what* actions we take. One thing is certain: if we continue to engage an analytic, linear, reductionistic approach, the resulting entropy and degradation will eventually grind our systems to a halt—and not just organizational systems but also the many systems in the organizational environment. The keys to the Systems Age are thus vital necessities on a widespread scale.

CONCLUSION

Many systems tools and aids are presented in this book. However, we must remember they are all based on four fundamental systems concepts:

1. The Seven Levels of Living (Open) Systems
2. The Laws of Natural Systems: Standard Systems Dynamics
3. The A-B-C-D Systems Model
4. Changing Systems: The Natural Cycles of Life and Change

We can use these four simple concepts to ensure we're staying on a systems-thinking track and moving *from chaos and complexity to elegant simplicity*. They and the 12 key systems questions are the beauty of systems thinking. We can use them as a quick start and reality check as well as a focus for our synergistic solution-seeking and visioning. If we remember to consistently pose systems questions first, and if we always remember that every system is an indivisible whole, we will be well on our way to discovering the secrets of the lost art of systems thinking and learning.

Bibliography

Aburdene, P. & Naisbitt, J. (1992). *Megatrends for Women*. NY: Villard Books.

Ackoff, R. (1974). *Redesigning the Future: A Systems Approach to Societal Problems*. NY: John Wiley & Sons, Inc.

Ackoff, R. (1991). *Ackoff's Fables: Irreverent Reflections on Business and Bureaucracy*. NY: John Wiley & Sons, Inc.

Argyris, C. & Schon, D. (1978). *Organizational Learning: A Theory of Action Perspective*. Reading, MA: Addison-Wesley.

Augros, R. M. & Stanciu, G. N. (1984). *The New Story of Science*. NY: Bantam Books.

Baker-Miller, J. (1976). *Toward a New Psychology of Women*. Boston, MA: Beacon Press.

Band, W. A. (1994). *Touchstones: Ten New Ideas Revolutionizing Business*. NY: John Wiley & Sons, Inc.

Barker, J. A. (1992). *The Future Edge: Discovering the New Paradigms of Success*. NY: William Morrow and Company, Inc.

Barlett, D. L. & Steele, J. B. (1992). *America: What Went Wrong?* Kansas City: MO: Andrews and McMeel.

Barry, R. (1993). *A Theory of Almost Everything*. Chatham, NY: Oneworld.

Bateson, G. (1980). *Mind and Nature*. NY: Bantam Books.

Bennis, W., Benne, R., Corey, C. & K. [Eds.]. (1976). *The Planning of Change*. NY: Holt, Rinehart and Winston.

Blank, W. (1995). *The 9 Natural Laws of Leadership*. NY: AMACOM Books.

Bohm, D. (1980). *Wholeness and the Implicate Order*. London: Ark Paperbacks.

Boulding, K. E. (1964). *The Meaning of the 20th Century*. NY: Prentice-Hall.

Briggs, J. & Peat, F. D. (1989). *Turbulent Mirror: An Illustrated Guide to Chaos Theory and the Science of Wholeness*. NY: Harper and Row.

Brinkerhoff, R. O. & Gill, S. J. (1994). *The Learning Alliance: Systems Thinking in Human Resource Development*. San Francisco: Jossey-Bass Publishers.

Bucholz, R. A. (1993). *Principles of Environmental Management: The Greening of Business*. NY: Prentice Hall.

Buckley, W. (1967). *Sociology and Modern Systems Theory*. NY: Prentice-Hall.

Capra, F. (1976). *The Tao of Physics*. NY: Bantam Books.

Capra, F. (1983). *The Turning Point: Science, Society and the Rising Culture*. NY: Bantam Books.

Carnevale, A. (1991). *America and the New Economy*. San Francisco: Jossey Bass Publishers.

Casti, J. L. (1994). *Complexification: Explaining a Paradoxical World Through the Science of Surprise*. NY: Harper Collins.

Chandler, A., Jr. (1962). *Strategy and Structure: Chapters in the History of the American Industrial Enterprise*. Cambridge, MA: The MIT Press.

Chopra, D. (1989). *Quantum Healing: Exploring the Frontiers of Mind and Body Science*. NY: Bantam Books.

Churchman, C. W. (1968). *The Systems Approach*. NY: Dell Publishing.

Coates, J. F. & Jarratt, J. (2nd printing 1990). *What Futurists Believe*. Bethesda, MD: The World Future Society.

Cohen, J. & Stewart I. (1994). *The Collapse of Chaos*. NY: The Penguin Group.

Colburn, T., Dumanoski, D. & Meyers, J. P. (1996). *Our Stolen Future*. NY: Dutton Signet.

Cornwell, J. [Ed.]. (1995). *Nature's Imagination*. Oxford University Press.

Covey, S. (1989). *The 7 Habits of Highly Effective People*. NY: Simon & Schuster.

Csanyi, V. (1989). *Evolutionary Systems and Society*. Durham, NC: Duke University Press.

Cummings, T. G. (1980). *Systems Theory for Organization Development*. NY: John Wiley & Sons.

Cummings, T. G. & Srivastva, S. (1977). *Management of Work: A Sociotechnical Systems Approach*. San Diego, CA: University Associates.

Cziko, G. (1995). *Without Miracles: Universal Selection Theory and the Second Darwinian Revolution*. Cambridge, MA: The MIT Press.

Davies, P. C. W. & Brown, J. (1988). *Superstrings: A Theory of Everything*? Cambridge, U.K.: Cambridge University Press.

Denton, D. K. (1991). *Horizontal Management: Beyond Total Customer Satisfaction*. NY: Lexington Books.

Dettmer, H. W. (1996). *Goldratt's Theory of Constraints*. Milwaukee, WI: ASQC Quality Press.

Diamond, I. & Orenstein, G. F. [Eds.]. (1990). *Reweaving the World: The Emergence of Ecofeminism*. San Francisco: Sierra Club Books.

Drucker, P. (1993). *Post-Capitalist Society*. NY: Harper Business.

Drucker, P. (1995). *Managing in a Time of Great Change*. NY: Dutton.

Duncan, W. L. (1994). *Manufacturing 2000*. NY: AMACOM Books.

Earley. J. (1997). *Transforming Human Culture—Social Evolution and the Planetary Crises*. Albany, NY: State University of New York Press.

Eberly, D. (1994). *Building a Community of Citizens*. Lanham, MD: University Press of America.

Eberly, D. (1994). *Restoring the Good Society: A New Vision for Politics and Culture*. Grand Rapids, MI: Baker Book House.

Eisler, R. (1987). *The Chalice and the Blade: Our History, Our Future*. San Francisco: Harper and Row.

Eisler, R. & Loye, D. (1990). *The Partnership Way: New Tools for Living and Learning*. San Francisco: Harper Collins.

Feininger, A. (1986). *In a Grain of Sand: Exploring Design by Nature*. San Francisco: Sierra Club Books.

Ferber, M. A. & Nelson, J. A. (1993). *Beyond Economic Man: Feminist Theory and Economics*. Chicago, IL: The University of Chicago Press.

Ferguson, K. (1994). *The Fire in the Equations: Science, Religion & the Search for God*. Grand Rapids, MI: Eerdmans.

Fombrun, C. J. (1992). *Turning Points: Creating Strategic Change in Corporations*. Los Angeles: R. R. Donnelly & Sons Company.

Forrester, J. W. (1969). *Urban Dynamics.* Norwalk, CT: Productivity Press.

Forrester, J. W. (1971) *World Dynamics (2nd ed.)*. Norwalk, CT: Productivity Press.

Forrester, J. W. (1971). *Principles of Systems*. Norwalk, CT: Productivity Press.

Forrester, J. W. (1971). *World Dynamics*. Cambridge, MA: Wright-Allen Press.

Forrester, J. W. (1975). *Collected Papers of Jay W. Forrester*. Norwalk, CT: Productivity Press.

Fox, M. & Shelldrake, R. (1996). *The Physics of Angels*. San Francisco: Harpers.

Frankel, V. (1959). *Man's Search for Meaning*. Boston, MA: Beacon Press.

Galbraith, J. R. (1993). *Organizing for the Future: The New Logic for Managing Complex Organizations*. San Francisco: Jossey-Bass Publishers.

Gell-Mann, M. (1995). *The Quark and the Jaguar*. NY: W. H. Freeman.

George, C. (1968). *The History of Management Thought*. Englewood Cliffs, NJ: Prentice Hall.

Glass, L. & Mackey, M. C. (1988). *From Clocks to Chaos*. Princeton, NJ: Princeton University Press.

Gleick, J. (1987). *Chaos: Making a New Science*. NY: Viking.

Goodman, M. R. (1974). *Study Notes in System Dynamics*. Norwalk, CT: Productivity Press.

Gore, A. (1993). *Earth in the Balance: Ecology and the Human Spirit*. NY: Penguin Books.

Griffin, S. (1982). *Made from This Earth*. NY: Harper and Row.

Haines, S. G. (1995). *Successful Strategic Planning*. Menlo Park, CA: Crisp Publications.

Haines, S. G. (1995). *Sustaining High Performance*. Delray Beach, FL: St. Lucie Press.

Hall, A. D. & Fagan, R. E. (1956). *Definition of System: General Systems 1.*

Hall, N. [Ed.]. (1994). *Exploring Chaos*. NY: W.W. Norton & Co.

Hamel, G. & Prahalad, C. K, (1994). *Competing for the Future*. Boston, MA: Harvard Business School Press.

Handy, C. (1989). *The Age of Unreason*. Cambridge, MA: Harvard Business School Press.

Handy, C. (1994). *The Age of Paradox*. Cambridge, MA: Harvard Business School Press.

Harman, W. & Hormann, J. (1990). *Creative Work: The Constructive Role of Business in a Transforming Society*. Indianapolis, IN: Knowledge Systems.

Hart, R. D. & Cooley, S. L. (1997). *A Nation Reconstructed*. Milwaukee, WI: ASQC Quality Press.

Hawken, P. (1993). *The Ecology of Commerce: A Declaration of Sustainability*. NY: Harper Business.

Heisenberg, W. (1958). *Physics and Philosophy*. NY: Harper Torchbooks.

Helgesen. S. (1990). *The Female Advantage: Women's Ways of Leadership*. NY: Doubleday.

Henderson, H. (1992). *Paradigms in Progress*. Indianapolis, IN: Knowledge Systems.

Henton, D., Melville, J. & Walesh, K. (1997). *Grassroots Leaders for a New Economy: How Civic Entrepreneurs Are Building Prosperous Communities*. San Francisco: Jossey-Bass Publishers.

Herbert, N. (1985). *Quantum Reality: Beyond the New Physics*. NY: Anchor Doubleday.

Herrnstein, R. J. & Murray, C. (1994). *The Bell Curve*. NY: Free Press.

Hickman, C., et al. *The Fourth Dimension*. NY: John Wiley & Sons.

Huntington, S. P. (1996). *The Clash of Civilizations and the Remaking of World Order*. NY: Simon and Schuster.

Itzkoff, S. W. (1994). *The Decline of Intelligence in America: A Strategy for National Renewal*. NY: Praeger.

Jantsch, E. (1975). *Design for Evolution: Self-Organization and Planning in the Life Human Systems*. NY: George Braziller, Inc.

Jantsch, E. (1980). *The Self-Organizing Universe*. Oxford: Pergamon Press.

Jaques, E. (1989). *Requisite Organization: The CEO's Guide to Creative Structure and Leadership*. Alexandria, VA: Cason Hall & Co. Publishers.

Johnson, R. A., Kast, F. E. & Rosenzweig, J. E. (1963). *The Theory and Management of Systems*. NY: McGraw-Hill.

Kaku, M. & Thompson, J. T. (1995). *Beyond Einstein (Revised)*. NY: Anchor Books.

Kanter, R. M. (1977). *Men and Women in the Corporation*. NY: Basic Books.

Kauffman, S. (1995). *At Home in the Universe*. NY: Oxford University Press.

Keil, L. D. (1994). *Managing Chaos and Complexity in Government: A New Paradigm for Managing Change, Innovation, Organizational Renewal*. San Francisco: Jossey-Bass Publishers.

Klir, G. (1969). *An Approach to General Systems Theory*. NY: Van Nostrand.

Klir, G. [Ed.]. (1972). *Trends in General Systems Theory*. NY: Wiley-Interscience.

Kuhn, T. (1970). *The Structure of Scientific Revolutions (2nd ed.)*. Chicago: University of Chicago Press.

Langdon, D. G. (1995). *The New Language of Work*. Amherst, MA: HRD Press.

Lanza, R. [Ed.] et al. (1996). *One World: The Health and Survival of the Human Species in the 21st Century*. Santa Fe, NM: Health Press.

Laszlo, E. (1972). *Introduction to Systems Philosophy*. NY: Gordon & Breach.

Laszlo, E. (1972). *The Systems View of the World*. NY: George Braziller.

Laszlo, E. (1994). *Vision 20/20*. Langhorne, PA: Gordon & Breach.

Laszlo, E. [Ed.]. (1991). *The New Evolutionary Paradigm*. NY: Gordon & Breach.

Lawler, E. E., III. (1992). *The Ultimate Advantage: Creating the High-Involvement Organization*. San Francisco: Jossey-Bass Publishers.

Lawler, E. E., III (1996). *From the Ground Up: Six Principles for Building New Logic Corporation*. San Francisco, CA: Jossey-Bass Publishers.

Lincoln, Y. S. [Ed.]. (1985). *Organizational Theory and Inquiry: The Paradigm Revolution*. Beverly Hills, CA: Sage.

Linstone, H. A. with Mitroff, I. I. (1994). *The Challenge of the 21st Century: Managing Technology and Ourselves in a Shrinking World*. NY: State University of New York Press.

Lovelock, J. E. (1987). *Gaia*. NY: Oxford University Press.

Lyman, F. (1990). *The Greenhouse Trap*. Boston, MA: Beacon Press.

Margenau, H. & Barghese, R. A. [Eds.]. (1992). *Cosmos, Bios, Theos*. La Salle, IL: Open Court.

Markley, O. W. & McCuan W. R. (1996). *America Beyond 2001: Opposing Viewpoints*. San Diego, CA: Greenhaven Press.

Martin, J. (1995). *The Great Transition*. NY: AMACOM

McNeill, D. & Freiberger, P. (1994). *Fuzzy Logic*. NY: Touchstone, Simon & Schuster.

Meadows, D., et al. (1979). *The Limits to Growth*. The Club at Rome.

Merchant, C. (1981). *The Death of Nature: Women, Ecology, and the Scientific Revolution*. San Francisco: Harper & Row.

Mesarovic, M. [Ed.]. (1967). *Views on General Systems Theory*. NY: John Wiley & Sons, Inc.

Miller, E. J. & Rice, A. K. (1967). *Systems of Organization*. London: Tavistock Publications.

Miller, E. L. (October 9165). *Living Systems: Basic Concepts*. Behavioral Science.

Mische, M. A. [Ed.]. (1996). *Reengineering: Systems Integration Success*. Boston, MA: Auerbach.

Montuori, A. & Conti. (1993). *From Power to Partnership*. San Francisco: Harper Collins.

Morrison, I. & Schmid, G. (1994). *Future Tense: The Business Realities of the Next Ten Years*. NY: William Morrow.

Nadler, G. & Hibino, S. (1994). *Breakthrough Thinking (Rev. 2nd ed.)*. Rocklin, CA: Prima Publishing.

Naisbitt, J. (1982). *Megatrends: Ten New Directions Transforming Our Lives*. NY: Warner.

Naisbitt, J. (1994). *Global Paradox: The Bigger the World Economy, the More Powerful Its Smallest Players*. NY: William Morrow.

Naisbitt, J. & Aburdene, P. (1986). *Reinventing the Corporation*. NY: Warner Books.

Naisbitt, J. & Aburdene, P. (1990). *Megatrends 2000: Ten New Directions for the 1990's*. NY: William Morrow and Company, Inc.

Nayak, P. R. & Ketteringham, J. M. (1993). *BREAKTHROUGH*. San Diego, CA: Pfeiffer & Company.

Nirenberg, J. (1993). *The Living Organization: Transforming Teams into Workplace Communities*. Homewood, IL: Business One Irwin.

Oshry, B. (1995). *Seeing Systems: Unlocking the Mysteries of Organizational Life*. San Francisco: Berrett-Koehler Publishers.

Peters, T. (1987). *Thriving on Chaos*. NY: Knopf.

Petersen, J. L. (1994). *The Road to 2015*. Corte Madera, CA: Waite Group Press.

Pfeiffer, J. W., Goodstein, L. D. & Nolan, T. M. (1989). *Shaping Strategic Planning: Frogs, Dragons, Bees and Turkey Tails*. San Diego, CA: Pfeiffer & Company.

Prigogine, I. & Stengers, I. (1984). *Order Out of Chaos*. NY: Bantam Books.

Quinn, D. (1992). *Ishmael*. NY: A Bantan/Turner Book.

Quinn, J. B. (1992). *Intelligent Enterprise: A Knowledge and Service Based Paradigm for Industry*. NY: The Free Press.

Ray, M. & Rinzler, A. [Eds.]. (1993). *The New Paradigm in Business: Emerging Strategies for Leadership and Organizational Change*. NY: Jeremy P. Tarcher/Perigee Books.

Richardson, G. P. (1991). *Feedback Thought in Social Science and Systems Theory*. Philadelphia, PA: University of Pennsylvania Press.

Roberts, E. B. [Ed.]. (1981). *Managerial Applications of System Dynamics*. Norwalk, CT: Productivity Press.

Ross, H. (1996). *Beyond the Cosmos*. Colorado Springs, CO: NAVPRESS.

Rothschild, M. (1990). *Bionomics: Economy as Ecosystem*. NY: Henry Holt & Co., Inc.

Rummler, G. & Brache, A. P. (1990). *Improving Performance*. San Francisco: Jossey-Bass Publishers.

Scarre, C. (1995). *Beyond Einstein: The Cosmic Quest for the Theory of Everything*. NY: Anchor.

Schneider, S. H. (1997). *Laboratory Earth: The Planetary Gamble We Can't Afford to Lose*. NY: Basic Books.

Senge, P. M. (1990). *The Fifth Discipline: The Art and Practice of the Learning Organization*. NY: Doubleday/Currency.

Senge, P. M., Roberts, C., Ross, R. B., Smith, B. J. & Kleiner, A. (1994). *The Fifth Discipline Field Book—Strategies and Tools for Building a Learning Organization*. NY: Doubleday/Currency.

Shrode, W. A. & Voich, D., Jr. (1974). *Organization and Management: Basic Systems Concepts*. Homewood, IL: Irwin, Inc.

Simon, H. A. (1957). *Models of Man*. NY: Wiley.

Sims, H. P. & Gioia, D. [Eds.]. (1986). *The Thinking Organization*. San Francisco: Jossey-Bass Publishers.

Stacey, R. D. (1992). *Managing the Unknowable: Strategic Boundaries between Order and Chaos*. San Francisco: Jossey-Bass Publishers.

Stead, E. & Stead, J. (1992). *Management for a Small Planet*. Newbury, CA: Sage.

Talbot, M. (1986). *Beyond the Quantum*. NY: Bantam Books.

Terry, R. (1995). *Economic Insanity*. San Francisco: Berrett-Koehler.

Theobald, R. (1992). *Turning the Century: Personal and Organizational Strategies for Your Changed World*. Indianapolis, IN: Knowledge Systems, Inc.

Toffler, A. (1970). *Future Shock*. NY: Random House.

Toffler, A. & Toffler, H. (1980). *The Third Wave*. NY: Bantam Books.

Toffler, A. & Toffler, H. (1995). *Creating a New Civilization: The Politics of The Third Wave*. Atlanta, GA: Turner Publishing, Inc.

Trist, E. & Emery, F. (1973). *Toward a Social Ecology*. London and NY: Plenum.

Vaill, P. B. (1996). *Learning as a Way of Being*. San Francisco: Jossey-Bass Publishers.

Vickers, G. (1970). *"A Classification of Systems": Yearbook of the Society for General Systems Research*. Washington, DC.

Volk, T. (1995). *Metapatterns*. NY: Columbia University Press.

Von Bertalanffy, L. (1968). *General Systems Theory*. NY: Braziller.

Waldrop, M. M. (1992). *Complexity: The Emerging Science at the Edge of Order and Chaos*. NY: Touchstone.

Wann, D. (1994). *Biologic: Designing with Nature to Protect the Environment (2nd ed.)*. Johnson Books.

Weinberg, S. (1992). *Dreams of a Final Theory*. NY: Pantheon Books.

Weisbord, M. (1992). *Discovering Common Ground*. San Francisco: Jossey-Bass Publishers.

Wheatley, M. J. (1994). *Leadership and the New Science*. San Francisco: Berrett-Koehler Publishers.

Wheatley, M. J. & Kellner-Rogers, M. (1996). *A Simpler Way*. San Francisco: Berrett-Koehler Publishers.

Wick, C. & Leon, L. S. (1993). *The Learning Edge: How Smart Managers and Smart Companies Stay Ahead*. NY: McGraw-Hill.

Wiener, N. (1961). *Cybernetics: Or Control and Communication in the Animal Machine (2nd ed.)*. Cambridge, MA: The MIT Press.

Wilbur, K. [Ed.]. (1985). *The Holographic Paradigm and Other Paradoxes*. Boulder, CO: Shambala Press.

Wilczek, F. & Devine, B. (1988). *Longing for the Harmonies*. NY: W. W. Norton and Co.

Wilson, E. O. & Kellert, S. R. [Eds.]. (1993). *The Biophilia Hypothesis*. Washington, DC: Island Press.

Wolf, F. A. (1988). *Parallel Universes*. NY: Touchstone Books.

Wolf, F. A. (1989). *Taking the Quantum Leap*. NY: Harper and Row.

Yankelovich, D. (1981). *New Rules*. NY: Random House.

Yankelovich, D. (1991). *Coming to Public Judgment: Making Democracy Work in a Complex World*. Syracuse, NY: Syracuse University Press.

Zohar, D. (1990). *The Quantum Self: Human Nature and Consciousness Defined by the New Physics*. NY: William Morrow and Co.

Zuboff, S. (1988). *In the Age of the Smart Machine*. NY: Basic Books.

Zukav, G. (1979). *The Dancing Wu Li Masters*. NY: Bantam Books.

About the Author

Stephen G. Haines has used systems thinking as his orientation to life since the late 1970s. He is currently president and founder of the Centre for Strategic Management® and an internationally recognized leader in strategic planning and strategic change. He has over 25 years of diverse international executive and consultant experience in virtually every part of both the private and public sectors.

Mr. Haines was formerly president and part owner of University Associates (UA) Consulting and Training Services. Prior to that, he was executive vice president and chief administrative officer of Imperial Corporation of America, a $13 billion nationwide financial services firm. He has been on eight top management teams with organization leadership for operations, planning, human resources, training, organization development, marketing, sales, communications, public relations, and facilities.

A 1968 U.S. Naval Academy (at Annapolis) engineering graduate with a foreign affairs minor, Mr. Haines has an Ed.D. (ABD) in management and educational psychology from Temple University and an M.S. in organization development from George Washington University.

Steve has written six books and eight volumes of the Centre's tool kits, guides and best practices (over 4000 pages), all based on systems thinking. He has taught over 60 different types of seminars and is in demand as a keynote speaker on CEO and Board of Director's issues. He has served on a number of boards and was chairman of the board for Central Credit Union in San Diego.

The Centre for Strategic Management® is an unusual mix of 12 master-level partners, consultants, and affiliates in the United States and Canada, with a growing number of master-consultant international affiliates in Australia, Korea, Turkey, South Africa, and Ireland.